easy
Closets

easy
Closets

AFFORDABLE STORAGE
SOLUTIONS FOR EVERYONE

Joseph R. Provey

CREATIVE HOMEOWNER®

EASY CLOSETS

PRODUCED BY	Home & Garden Editorial Services
PROJECT MANAGER	Joe Provey
COPY EDITOR	Owen Lockwood
INDEXER	Home & Garden Editorial Services
INTERIOR DESIGN CONCEPT	Kathryn Wityk, David Geer
COVER DESIGN	David Geer
ILLUSTRATIONS	Vince Babak (page 98)
FRONT COVER PHOTOGRAPHY	*Main image* courtesy of The Container Store; *top left* courtesy of Shulte Corp.; *top middle* courtesy of The Container Store; *top right* iStockphoto
BACK COVER PHOTOGRAPHY	*Top* courtesy of Shulte Corp.; *bottom left* courtesy of California Closets; *bottom middle* courtesy of IKEA; *bottom right* courtesy of Shulte Corp.

Manufactured in Singapore

Current Printing (last digit)
10 9 8 7 6

Easy Closets, First Edition
Library of Congress Control Number: 2009940486
ISBN 978-1-58011-489-9

Creative Homeowner®, *www.creativehomeowner.com*, is an imprint of New Design Originals Corporation and distributed in North America by Fox Chapel Publishing, 800-457-9112, 1970 Broad Street, East Petersburg, PA 17520, and in the UK by Grantham Book Service, Trent Road, Grantham, Lincolnshire, NG31 7XQ.

Dedication

To MaryAnn, my wonderfully disorganized wife, and our seven kids: Tara, Kenny, Joseph, Ren, Corinna, Thomas, and Cailee. Kids, please come and take your stuff out of the basement so we can do some much-needed organization ourselves!

Acknowledgments

Many thanks to interior designer Donna Striebe of C&S Interiors LLC for reading the manuscript, offering many helpful suggestions, and even finding the occasional spelling error and grammatical mistake. Thanks, too, to designer Lars Dalsgaard, who shared several of his original designs for the book—all carefully conceived so that just about anyone who can wield a hammer and a screwdriver can build them. Lisa Adams of LA Closet Design offered insights not only about better ways to store things but also about the importance people place on the appearance and comfort of their closets. Lauren Spahr and Betty Schmal, designers at Rubbermaid, expertly answered many of my questions about the materials with which closet systems are manufactured and how to use them to design just the right closet for the space and location. Special thanks also go to Lisa Lennard of California Closets for her insights about closet trends and to Cathy Brennan, the Connecticut owner of a California Closets franchise who graciously allowed us to tour her showroom and fabrication workshop. Finally, a big thanks to editor Owen Lockwood for his dedication to producing the best possible books. This is the 10th book we've done together for Creative Homeowner.

Contents

8 Introduction

CHAPTER ONE

10 **Simplify, and Then Reorganize**
11 Pare Down Your Possessions
14 Put It Where You Use It...
19 Using All the Space
20 Good Lighting Is Essential

CHAPTER TWO

22 **Components and Systems**
23 Shelving: Fast, Easy, Inexpensive
24 Poles and Rods
29 Pegs and Hooks
30 Pullout Trays
32 Drawers and Cabinets
33 Custom Closets
36 Closet Systems

CHAPTER THREE

44 **Coat Closets and Mudrooms**
45 Winning Back Your Coat Closet
46 At the Front Door
49 At the Back Door
53 Making Room for Kids

CHAPTER FOUR

54 **Kids' Closets**
55 Closets That Grow with Your Child
61 Older Kids' Closets

CHAPTER FIVE

66 **Master-Suite Closets**
67 To Share or Not to Share
68 Will It All Fit?
70 Fitting in the Rest
73 Reach-in Closets
78 Walk-in Closets
82 Off-Season Clothing Storage
83 Create a Guest Closet

CHAPTER SIX

84 **Linen Closets**
85 Table Linens
86 Bed and Bath Linens

CHAPTER SEVEN

92 **Kitchen Pantries**
93 Walk-in, Reach-in, and Cabinet Pantries
97 Pantry Storage Strategies
102 Pantry Drawers
104 Where the Wine Lives

CHAPTER EIGHT

106 **Closets on a Budget**
107 The Freestanding Solution
109 Building Your Own Wardrobe
112 Creating "Closets" Out of Thin Air
115 Over the Door

CHAPTER NINE

116 **Utility, Garage, and Basement Closets**
117 Utility Closets: Function Over Fancy
120 Garages and Basements
124 Outdoor "Closets"

CHAPTER TEN

126 **Closets That Do More**
127 Specialty Closets
134 Rooms in a Closet

CHAPTER ELEVEN

136 **Closets Where There Were None**
137 Adding a New Closet
142 Framing Basics
144 Drywall Basics
146 Hinged Door Basics
149 Finding "Leftover" Spaces for Closets

150 Resource Guide
154 Glossary
156 Index
158 Credits

Introduction

CLOSETS CONJURE UP LOTS OF IMAGES. They can be frightening. My kid brother thought a witch lived in the closet in the childhood bedroom we shared. She drove a small red car. Some of us keep skeletons in our closets, while others strive to step out of closets and live fuller lives. In storybooks, children disappear into closets and find passageways to new worlds.

There is not a lot written about the history of the closet. One source suggests that the first closets were hollowed-out logs. This makes some sense because hollowed logs have been used for everything from canoes to cribs. As woodworking tools and skills evolved, and as storage needs became greater, the hollowed log gave way to the wooden chest. It's not difficult to see the modern housewife of the Dark Ages wanting the latest in convenience—a lidded enclosure!

At some point, that lidded enclosure was stood on end and became a vertical chest. As with many advances in technology, it may have been prompted by warfare. The armoire, after all, was first a place to store weaponry. Vertical chests for hanging and storing folded clothing were not far behind. Eventually, the more genteel name, "wardrobe," became the preferred term. And so it went for centuries: people stored items in wardrobes equipped with doors, shelves, hooks, and perhaps a drawer if you were well off.

THE EARLIEST WALK-IN "CLOSETS"

As the middle class grew, some people needed big wardrobes—big enough to walk into. In fact, in seventeenth-century Europe the closet or "cabinet" was a private room, often behind the bedroom, that was filled with books and works of art. It functioned as a sitting room, office, or studio. There could be more than one closet in the house, each serving only one individual. A closet for a woman was sometimes called a "boudoir."

Designer closets were once a luxury. With today's organizing systems, however, an efficient, beautiful closet is possible for every budget. Whether you want to bring order to your foyer closet (left), to upgrade a shared walk-in closet (opposite top), or to use closet organizers to store materials in a craft or sewing room (opposite bottom), *Easy Closets* is filled with dozens of great design ideas and accessories.

NEW TRENDS

Homeowners are beginning to realize that simple is better. Today's green movement promotes recycling instead of always buying new. Online auctions and classified services make it easier than ever to resell used items you no longer need. Technology has made it possible to store many items in very small places: entire libraries of books and movies, not to mention games, now fit in the palm of your hand. The old-fashioned notion of sharing has also gained some traction of late, too. In many cities, for example, you can join a car-sharing network so you don't need to own—or store—one yourself.

Closets are also moving out of dark corners into open rooms. As shown in *Easy Closets*, "open" closets have no walls or doors. Closet organizing components hang from walls near entryways, in home offices, in garages and basements, and elsewhere.

Regardless of what form the closet takes in the future, it will remain an important part of the home. I hope this book opens your eyes to the many possibilities and products available today to make the most of the closets you have. I also hope it impresses upon you that closet reorganization is only half the battle. Just as important is the need to jettison items you no longer need, and to do so in a way that is not wasteful and, ideally, helps others.

MORE MONEY, MORE STUFF

When the prosperity generated by the Industrial Revolution began to take hold in the nineteenth century, more people were able to afford more clothing and other items, such as tools, utensils, and dinnerware. They needed places in the home to put them. Closets, as we know them today, began to show up more often in the houses of the wealthy. At the beginning of the twentieth century, closets had become a must-have for the middle class as well. In fact, one theory suggests that the migration to the suburbs from cities in the twentieth century was, in part, driven by the desire for closets!

The trend to more and bigger closets has continued in recent decades. Reach-in closets are no longer the envy of your neighbors. It's the walk-in closet that gets the oohs and aahs. As with the kitchen, it has become something of a showplace. If you spend a lot of money on nice cloths and footwear, why store them in a dark and dusty closet? These walk-in spaces are filled with cabinetry, good lighting, and even chandeliers and silk-upholstered lounges.

Where we go next is a matter of some debate. It's likely that new houses will be smaller in the future than they were in the heady days of McMansions and Hummers. Smaller houses will require smarter organization, including better-designed closets that utilize the concepts described in this book.

Simplify, and Then Reorganize

Chapter 1

NO MATTER HOW BIG OR HOW MANY closets you have, they alone cannot solve your storage needs. Without thinking through what you need and what you don't, you will be doomed to a life of disorder and inefficiency, and to wasting a lot of time and money. For these reasons, we begin with important advice on getting rid of the things you don't need—and a simple approach to organizing the things you do.

By avoiding overcrowding, it's easier to find your things. After all, if you can't find what you own, it's not much different than not having it.

Smart Tip

It may be counterintuitive, but good places to begin when reorganizing your closets are in the attic, garage, and basement. This is typically where you'll want to store bulk supplies and items that don't get used regularly but that you can't do without.

Pare Down Your Possessions

Admittedly, it's not easy to pare down. It's difficult to give away the set of dishes your mom gave you, even if you never use them. How about the sports jacket—which no longer fits—that you spent most of your first paycheck on? We often have emotional attachments to things. Some say that their possessions make them feel good—even when it's clear that they are no longer useful. They rationalize that perhaps they—or some other family member—will need the things someday. In my experience, possessions are not what good mental health should depend on, and "someday" almost invariably never comes.

Remodeling a closet—or building a new one—is not in-expensive. You can spend $100 per square foot, especially if your design includes drawers. So the last thing you want to do is to waste money storing items you no longer use. Unless you're planning to make a killing 30 years from now selling vintage clothing, magazines, toys, and the like, go through your closets and remove the following three types of items.

1. Stuff you don't use. If you haven't used it for more than one or two years, get rid of it. Focus on things such as clothing, old electronics, and kitchen gadgets. Pull dated foodstuffs from the pantry. Why are you saving your old film

Wall-hung utility shelving in the garage or basement is a good way to reduce demands on your household closets.

camera and all its lenses even though you've gone digital and never intend to use film again? Each item, by itself, may not look as if it consumes much space, but taken together, they can easily fill a closet or two or three!

When sorting clothing, portable racks are helpful. For other items, use packing boxes, and do your sorting in a spare room or the garage.

2. Bulk supplies. Buying items that you use every day, such as paper towels, toilet paper, tissues, and canned goods, in bulk is a great way to save money. Just don't use up prime closet space to store it all. Select what you need for the next few weeks, and earmark the rest for "long-term parking" in a spare hallway closet, under a staircase, or in the attic, the basement, or the garage.

3. Stuff you use a few times a year. You may only need these items two or three times a year. Nevertheless, you can't do without them. Formal dresses and tuxedos, punch bowls, and large serving platters fall into this category for many of us.

TAKING ACTION!

Give the first pile away. If you don't have kids, nieces, or nephews to foist the stuff on, bring it to Goodwill or a similar charity. (Don't forget to take a receipt. It may come in handy as a deduction at tax time.) If the items are worth too much to give away, you can try selling them at a consignment shop or a tag sale, through the classifieds, or on the Internet. Store the remaining piles in the garage, attic, or basement. Build or purchase utility shelving for

Go Digital and Save Shelf Space

Living in the iEra—with iPads, iPods, Kobos, Kindles, Nooks, and the like—has made it possible to store enormous numbers of books, music, movies, photo albums, games, personal contacts, and business and personal files in almost no space at all. Pay your bills online, and you'll no longer need file drawers filled with records. Collect Web sites that do a good job with recipes, and chuck all but your favorite cookbooks.

You don't, of course, need to get rid of everything. Reduce your storage footprint to only meaningful items that you may want to handle and peruse from time to time—perhaps a set of art books, a wedding album, or favorite movies you like to watch regularly. Using these electronic "closets" makes good sense, but be sure to back up your material on a hard drive or online storage service. The former costs about $60 (for a 500 GB external hard drive). The latter costs about $10 to $20 per month for 100 GB—and you don't have to worry about any data being lost or stolen. Too bad you can't back up your jewelry!

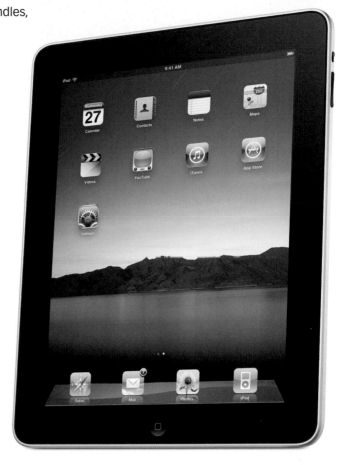

infrequently used kitchenware and bulk supplies of paper goods and foodstuffs. Buy portable racks or hanger bags for clothing. Store smaller garments in clear plastic bins with lids. Of course, if you're blessed with bountiful closets, choose the one that's least needed and put bulk supplies and rarely used items there.

DON'T BE A DUPE

Now go back through your closets one more time, and then focus on duplicates. Sure, you "need" sheets, but do you need 10 sets of them? My wife and I recently pulled out five sets of sheets from our overstuffed linen closet that we hadn't used for years. Do you really need 18 juice glasses, six potholders, four corkscrews, three spatulas, and two waffle irons? Coats and jackets consume a lot of space. Do

you really need all of them? I recently heard of a man with 500 T-shirts!

Clothes closets are typically the worst. (By the way, this goes for dressers, too.) Sure, you need sweatshirts, but do you need 10 of them? If you do your laundry once a week, three or four is plenty. Same goes for undergarments, dress shirts, jeans, T-shirts, shoes, and boots. If you can thin out your wardrobe, storing it is going to be less expensive and a lot easier—and so will finding the blouse or shoes you need to complete an outfit while you're rushing off to work on Monday morning.

Once you've thinned out your possessions based on the few simple steps outlined above, you'll not only be able to find things faster but you'll get more pleasure from daily activities, including dressing and cooking.

Whether it's a broom or a bracelet, store items near where you use them most frequently. Jewelry (right) goes where you get dressed. So does the fold-out ironing board (below). And what better place for a mirror than where you check out your outfit or knot your tie (opposite, center)? This pullout puts a handy mirror right where you need it. The mirror folds flat (opposite, left) against the side of the closet when not in use.

Put It Where You Use It...

Let's not make closet design more complicated than it is. If you were to build a new house, you'd put closets close to where you use the stored items. Linen closets would go near bathrooms, broom closets and pantries near the kitchen, coat and boot closets near an entrance, game and craft closets near the family room, and clothing and bedding closets adjacent to the bedroom. The same goes if, as is usually the case, the closets have already been built. Choose the closet closest to the anticipated activity to store items related to that activity. Kitchens are the scene of the most frequent cleaning activity, so store cleaning equipment as close by as possible. If you like to sew, store your machine and supplies in a closet near where you sew.

If there's not enough room for sheets, quilts, and pillow cases in a bedroom closet, perhaps you can use part of a hallway closet or guest bedroom closet to store them. Not all homes have the perfect arrangement, but we make do.

Don't think twice about storing odd bedfellows in the same closet. It's fine to combine vacuum cleaner (and filter bags) and bathroom towel storage in a hallway closet, if doing so makes your life a little easier, or to keep an ironing board in a bedroom closet, near where you dress. A combination that has worked well for me over the years is to keep a toolbox in the kitchen broom closet. Storing a basic assortment of tools in the kitchen eliminates dozens of trips to the basement or the garage in the course of a year.

Put cleaning tools and supplies closest to where you need them most frequently. The kitchen (below) is typically where the mess is!

...BUT DON'T FORGET TO MOVE IT

Some items, of course, do not get used year-round. You don't need a lobster pot in the kitchen in winter. Nor do you need to store winter coats nearby in summer. At the beginning of each season, get in the habit of moving items from high-priority storage to low-priority storage and vice versa. Items that should be moved at least twice a year, and which many homeowners forget about, include the following: seasonal clothing, snow-removal equipment, air conditioners and fans, flannel sheets, humidifiers and dehumidifiers, and fireplace equipment and kindling.

Once you're organized, you won't want to go back to the confusion of the past. Once every six months or at the very least once a year, go through your items and weed out what you no longer need.

Smart Tip

Store like with like. This simple but often neglected rule of organization will help you find things faster. For example, separate tops by color— blues, blacks, browns, whites, and so forth. That way you won't have to rummage as much to find the top you want. It works in other closets, too: put all of your drill bits together in one organizer; put all canned tomato products on one shelf, and so on.

A Closet in Five Ways

1 **Freestanding closets.** Traditional freestanding closets go by many names, including wardrobes, chifforobes, and armoires, and they typically have hinged doors. Inside, there may be rods, shelves, drawers, or some combination thereof.

Contemporary freestanding closets, also called "wardrobes," are usually positioned against a wall but can be anchored to the floor anywhere to form a room divider in a large room. They have two or more sliding doors that are often mirrored or covered with fabric. Many manufacturers offer specialty components, including shoe racks, hampers, and jewelry trays. Footprints range from about 15 x 40 inches to 26 x 120 inches. Heights range from 6 to nearly 8 feet. Prices range from a few hundred dollars to thousands, depending on size, fittings, materials, and finish.

2 **Roll-out, fold-out, and rotating closets.** Often found in kitchens, they allow the user to pull stored contents into the room, making it easier to see everything at a glance. They rely upon sturdy hardware that ranges from slides for pullout shelving to C-shaped frames and rollers that allow you to pull the contents of an entire closet into the room.

3 **Walk-in closets.** Walk-in closets are usually found adjacent to bedrooms and kitchens, where they are called "pantries." Near bedrooms, walk-ins are typically composed of a combination of closet rods, drawers, pullouts, shelves, cubbies, and racks arranged on two or three walls with an aisle down the center. In kitchens, walk-in pantries are primarily made up of shelving and drawers,

along with some hooks for aprons and brooms. Overall dimensions of walk-in bedroom closets and kitchen pantries vary, but 6 x 8 feet is typical. Walk-in closets may also be found in finished attics and basements. If you're converting either one to living space, be sure to reserve at least a 10 x 10-foot area for storage.

4 **Reach-in closets.** Reach-in closets are what most of us grew up with. They are recesses in the wall that are enclosed with a door or doors. Reach-ins are typically 2 feet deep and 6 or 7 feet wide. Those that are composed of only a rod and shelf above are prime candidates for reorganization because much of the space above and below the hung clothing is wasted or difficult to get access to.

5 **Open closets.** Organizing systems have made their way out of closets into rooms. Dubbed "open" closets, they are typically found in basements and garages but may also be used for toys and office and craft supplies.

> **Closet Fact:** There were very few closets in Colonial America, even in well-to-do homes. This was due to taxes that were assessed based upon the number of rooms in a house—and closets counted as rooms. Instead, wall pegs, shelves, wardrobes, trunks, and clothing poles with hanger arms were used.

Using Space from Top to Bottom

1 **Adding a second top shelf**, and maintaining organization with baskets or vertical dividers, makes good use of space that's typically underutilized and prone to messiness. You may have to lower your closet rod to accommodate the second shelf.

2 **Doubling up your closet poles** is a smart way to better use the area near the ceiling of a closet. Hardware is available that allows you to pull the upper pole down to within easy reach. (See page 25.)

3 **Using hooks** in closet recesses or on doors is a good way to store frequently used items, such as bathrobes, aprons, handbags, umbrellas, belts, and hats.

4 **Off-the-floor, pullout racks** are the ideal way to store shoes: they're easy to see, there's good air circulation, and you can vacuum under them.

5 **Bins mounted on drawer slides** or casters are a good way to use space at the bottom of closets, especially closets with wide openings. Baskets may, of course, be placed directly on the floor, but they will make vacuuming chores more difficult.

6 **Sidewalls of freestanding closets** can host a multitude of organizers in very little space. This pullout rack holds ties, belts, and a tray for personal items you need every day.

Another good way to use high spaces is with vertical dividers. As long as you can reach the bottom of the compartment, you can pull down tall items stored there. Boxes, boots, blankets, pillows, and sheets can all be stored vertically. So can laundered shirts that have been folded and backed with cardboard. In kitchen pantries, vertical dividers are ideal for serving trays and paper bags. Vertical dividers can be built into the shelving (left) or clipped on (below).

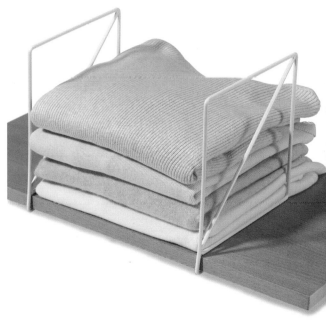

Using All the Space

Most of us think of closets in terms of linear feet, as in how long is the closet pole? But when considering a closet remodeling, it's better to think in terms of cubic feet. Right away you'll see space that, with the right organizers, you can begin to use. It's not uncommon to increase usable storage space by 35 percent. When redesigning a closet, the challenge is to use all of the space, including areas near the ceiling, the floor, the sides, the back, and behind the door—and to still be able to find items easily. Just don't overdo it. Closets need to "breathe," and you have to be able to see stored items quickly and easily.

Saving MONEY

Over-the-door organizers are a low-cost way to add storage to any closet with a hinged door. They can handle everything from shoes and sandals to gift wrap and baseball caps. Over-the-door handbag organizers (left) are very popular. Go to jokari.com for other options.

Smart Tip

Don't get too creative with colors when it comes to closet interiors. Stick with light tones. The surfaces will bounce light onto the items you store there, making them easier to see—and find.

For a small walk-in closet, choose a fluorescent surface-mounted fixture with a translucent cover. It will illuminate a full 360°.

Good Lighting Is Essential

Your closet organization may be brilliant, but if the lighting isn't, you'll still spend more time searching for items than you should. Many reach-in closets have only a single overhead light. It's of limited value because shelves and closet poles end up shading the lower part of the closet. To improve on the in-closet light, add one or two recessed ceiling fixtures outside the closet about 2 feet from the doors. Avoid placing them too far into the room; otherwise, you will cast shadows on stored items as you search for them. Some people use battery-powered puck lights as an inexpensive alternative to wired lighting; unfortunately, most units don't contribute enough light to be very helpful.

In a large walk-in closet, install two or more recessed lights per storage wall, depending on the size of the closet. Choose adjustable fixtures that allow you to aim the light to where it's needed. Place the fixtures directly over where you will stand when searching for items so that you will not cast a shadow on them.

LIGHTING SAFETY

Closets have a way of becoming overstuffed, but jamming that last item onto the top shelf and forcing the door closed is bad organization *and* may pose a fire hazard. That's because lights can get hot enough to ignite fabric, especially

For convenience and energy savings, you can mount wireless occupancy sensors on the ceiling to control walk-in closet lighting. No wiring is necessary, but you must replace existing light switches with compatible ones. Use where wired sensors are difficult to install.

Solar tubes or optical cables can funnel natural light into enclosed spaces, such as walk-in closets. Add-on electric lighting kits are available for solar tubes so you have light even when it's dark outside. Dimmer baffles are also available.

Climate Control

In closets where humidity is high, use a small dehumidifier. For most closets, a desiccant/silica gel-style dehumidifier works fine. Just hang it from the closet pole. When the indicator shows it must be recharged, plug it into any electrical outlet, and it will begin to absorb moisture once again. For persistent humidity, a drying rod (reduces humidity with mild heat) or a small conventional dehumidifier may be suitable.

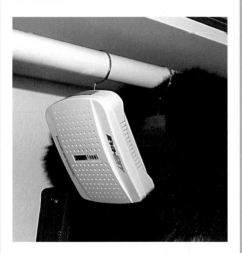

if you have an incandescent fixture. Replace fixtures that expose or partially expose incandescent lightbulbs. Ditto for pendant fixtures or pull-chain bulb holders. For other fixtures, observe the minimum clearances specified by the National Electrical Code. (See the table at right.)

SWITCH OPTIONS

Switches are best located outside the closet on the wall. Install one with a light-on indicator so you can see whether the light is on. Some automatic switches are triggered by opening and closing the door. Others are activated by motion sensors.

Closet Lighting Clearances

FIXTURE	LOCATION	INCHES FROM STORAGE
Incandescent and LED with enclosed sources	Surface mounted on wall or on ceiling	12
Fluorescent	Surface mounted on wall or on ceiling	6
Recessed incandescent or LED, enclosed source	In the wall or ceiling	6
Recessed fluorescent	In the wall or ceiling	6
Fluorescent or LED	Surface mounted	0*

If identified for this use.

Components and Systems

Chapter 2 **CLOSET ORGANIZATION RELIES** on an assortment of components, including rods, shelves, pegs, hooks, cabinets, drawers, and pullout trays, bins, and racks. Components can be built in a shop or purchased individually or as part of a ready-to-assemble system in which the components have been engineered to work together. No matter which approach you choose, select components that will best serve your needs.

Laminates resist shelf wear and make surfaces easy to keep clean, but a couple of coats of enamel paint or varnish on wood or plywood will also give you an easy-to-clean surface.

Shelving: Fast, Easy, Inexpensive

Shelving is the quickest and least expensive way to improve the organization of a closet. It can be made of wire, fiberboard, plywood, solid wood, or glass. All have their pluses. Wire shelves promote circulation and visibility, and don't collect dust. They are easy to install, either with rail-hung standards, wall braces, or steel posts.

Prefinished fiberboard shelves work well for short spans of 2 feet or less. They are usually covered with a laminate or a less durable glued-on paper and a coat of polyure-thane. Fiberboard shelves are typically supported by vertical dividers. The dividers have predrilled holes for shelving pegs that allow you to easily adjust shelf heights to suit your needs. Fiberboard shelves may also be supported by wall brackets or rail-hung standards, which are slotted to accept brackets. (See page 42.)

Wood or plywood shelves can span longer distances than fiberboard or wire shelves without sagging—a consideration when storing heavy items. They, too, may be supported by vertical dividers or brackets that are either wall-mounted or rail-and-standard-mounted. For heavy loads, the shelves are typically permanently joined to plywood or solid wood dividers. Cleats or dadoes provide the support. For glass shelves, rail-hung standards and brackets are a popular choice.

Improving upon the Basic Shelf

Shelving by itself is only half the answer to smart storage. That's because items stored at the back of a shelf are often hidden by what is in front. Shelves also encourage "piling" of items. Picture a pile of a dozen sheets on a shelf. Now try to pull out the set on the bottom.

Shelving is vastly improved with the use of bins, baskets, and boxes. Fiber baskets are nice, but even a cardboard box will do. Another way to organize shelves is with dividers, vertical components that divide shelves into segments. They keep piles of bulky sweaters from spilling over adjacent items. With many systems, dividers clamp in place and can be arranged to suit your needs.

Cubbies and shelf dividers are good ways to keep items from sliding around and piling up on one another.

Wire half-shelves enable you to use space that might otherwise be wasted, as is often the case with fixed shelves.

Slightly angled shelves improve visibility, especially for shelves below waist level.

Poles and Rods

Poles are available in wood or metal (in which case they are sometimes called "rods"). Wooden poles, called "round stock," come in 1¼- and 1⅜-inch diameters (actual dimensions). Choose the latter unless the span is short. Wooden poles may be stained or painted to match the surrounding trim, with the former holding up better to wear.

Metal rods, made of steel or aluminum, come in round 1-, 1¼-, and 1⁵⁄₁₆-inch diameters. Choose the latter for heavy loads. They come in chrome, brass, oil-rubbed bronze, satin nickel, and white finishes. Rod sockets are finished to match. Other rods have oblong profiles that add strength. Both wooden and metal poles are supported at both ends

A quick way to double the pole in your closet is to hang a second, shorter rod from the first. Buy sturdy units only, and avoid kits with spot-welded joints. Or make your own with strapping, chain, or cord and eyehooks. Keep in mind that you may have to add support to the top pole to prevent sagging.

Many closet companies now offer pull-down closet rods that allow you to access items hung on high rods. The hinged rods are easy to raise and lower with a pull handle (below).

by wood, plastic, or metal sockets (also called "flanges"). It is best to mount flanges to wooden cleats that are fastened to studs, not just to drywall.

Some metal rods are telescoping, so you can adjust them to the width of your closet without having to cut them to length. They come in a variety of width ranges, including 30–48 inches, 48–72 inches, and 72–120 inches, and sometimes have factory-attached flanges. Brackets may also be used to support closet poles and rods, in which case the ends are capped.

There's not a great deal of difference between metal rods and wooden poles in terms of their load-bearing capacities. In either case, if the rod or pole deflection is more than ½ inch, it's wise to limit the load or add extra support to reduce spans.

Load Capacity Comparison for Rods and Poles

TYPE	SPAN IN FEET	DEFLECTION AT 40 POUNDS
1¼-in. wood	3	¼ in.
1⅜-in. wood	3	⅛ in.
1-in. steel	3	⅜ in.
1¼-in. steel	3	1/16 in.
1⅜-in. wood	6	¾ in.
1¼-in. steel	6	⅝ in.

Results may vary based upon gauge of steel and species of wood

Getting the Hang of It

If you're thinking about reorganizing your clothes closets, you'll probably want to upgrade your old collection of mismatched hangers, too. Today's hangers look great, resist slipping and creasing better, and are even greener. Experts say that if you use the proper hangers, you can extend the life of your favorite garments. Here is some information about different hanger types to help you make the right choices.

Wooden hangers (above) come in many styles and finishes, including mahogany and cherry. Wide ones are good for suits, jackets, and gowns because they maintain the shape of clothing at the shoulders. Some have notches in the shoulder area to hold strapped garments in place and keep clothes from slipping. Others have extra bars or stretch bands that keep slacks from slipping. Avoid hanging sweaters. They can easily sag and develop the dreaded "shoulder hump."

Eco-friendly hangers include those made from bamboo and wheat. Both are compostable.

Plastic hangers incorporate many of the features of wood hangers and are economical. They come in every color of the rainbow, too. Some have built-in belt hooks.

Velvet flocked hangers (used with a cascading hanger, right) do a great job of preventing clothes from slipping. They're also narrow, so they conserve space.

Wire hangers are usually flimsy, ugly, and slippery. They also have a habit of getting tangled together and springing off clothing rods. Keep a few on hand for craft projects, and recycle the rest.

Padded hangers (right) are good for lingerie and other delicate garments.

Specialty hangers and hanger accessories are sometimes helpful. Two of the most popular types of specialty hangers are tiered and cascading. The former allows you to hang several items—often pairs of pants—on one hanger. The latter (below) is for hanging shirts. Hang both ends of the cascading hanger on the rod; hang clothes hangers on the allotted slots; and drop one end. It's a true space-saver. Other hangers are available specifically for scarves, belts, and ties. Plastic shoulder covers protect the tops of items from dust.

Standard sizes for adult hangers are as follows: 15 in. for petites, 17 in. for adults. Oversized hangers can be used for suits and coats, but you don't want to use a hanger that's too wide to handle standard shirts.

Options: Shelf and Rod Brackets

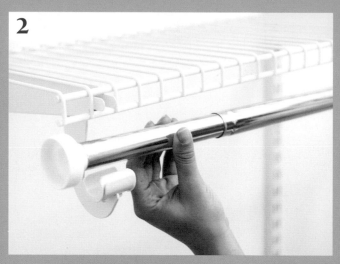

1 **Shelving hardware** typically uses a wall for support. With this system, however, sturdy panels are attached to the wall first, and the components are attached to hardware behind the panels through small slots.

2 **Stud locations** are not always where you need them to be. This system solves that with a horizontal support rail. First, you fasten the rail to studs every 16 inches; then you hang the notched standards (verticals) on the rail as needed without regard to stud location. Although you go on to fasten the standards to the wall using screws and anchors, it's the rail that carries the load. You may then attach rod hangers to the shelf brackets as shown. The rods simply snap in place.

3 **This shelf and rod bracket** gets fastened directly to a stud using 2-inch wood screws. You will also join the bracket and shelf to each other using screws. To find wall studs, you can use an electronic stud finder or a finishing nail and hammer. Simply drive the nail into the drywall at intervals until you hit a stud. The next stud will be 16 inches away.

Pegs and hooks are popular closet components, especially on the front or back of a hinged door. They are also great near entryways where they will support wet garments. Shaker-style peg racks (left) are perfect for a mudroom. A brass-plated double hook (below) can be found in any home-improvement center.

Pegs and Hooks

Before closet poles and shelves, there were pegs and hooks. Perhaps the most convenient type of storage because of how easy they are to use, pegs and hooks are still popular today. Install them on closet walls, the front or back of hinged doors, and walls where there is no space for a full closet. They are also great in mudrooms, where you can hang wet garments in the open while they dry.

Install pegs and hooks individually or grouped on a panel, in which case they become a rack. The latter requires far fewer holes in the wall to install. Make panels long enough so that they can be mounted to at least two wall studs, which are typically spaced 16 inches apart from stud center to stud center.

Saving MONEY

You can make your own hat and clothing pegs using tree branches. Simply cut several young branches from a hardwood tree and fashion them into pegs. Bore a row of holes of similar diameter into a 1x4 board. Whittle the branch ends to fit; glue them in place; and apply varnish.

In the "before" photo, retrieving items stored at the back of the cabinet was a nuisance. In the "after" shot, everything is within easy reach.

AFTER

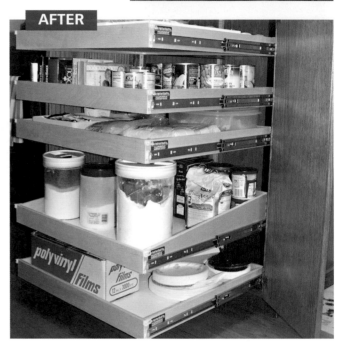

Revolving shelves are an alternative to pullouts, even though a small amount of storage space is wasted between the circular shelves and the cabinet corners. They are especially suitable for corners.

Pullout Trays

Pullout trays, sometimes referred to as pullout shelves, offer advantages similar to drawers. They allow you to pull stored items into the room where you can see them. They make the most of pantry or closet space because, unlike fixed shelves, there is no need to allow clearance above stored items for access. You can choose units with low fronts and sides for better visibility and easier lifting or with deep sides to keep items corralled. Pullouts are available in solid wood, plywood, wire, or a combination of wire and wood. Avoid pullouts made with particleboard, although a hardboard base is OK. Figure on spending about $30 per tray, including hardware. Pullouts tend to be less expensive than drawers. They do not require a cabinet front (rails and stiles) or fancy false fronts and pull hardware. Pullout racks are available for pants, ties, shoes, and belts.

How To: Install a Pullout Tray or Shelf

Installing a pullout tray in a closet, or in a kitchen base cabinet as shown here, is a project that even a beginner can finish in an hour or two. Order trays that are 1 inch narrower than the closet or cabinet opening and about an inch shorter (less deep) than the cabinet depth.

Note that some cabinet doors, when open, may interfere with tray movement because they project slightly into the opening. If that is the case, order a tray width that will clear the doors, and use shims (visible in photo 2 below) to position slides as necessary.

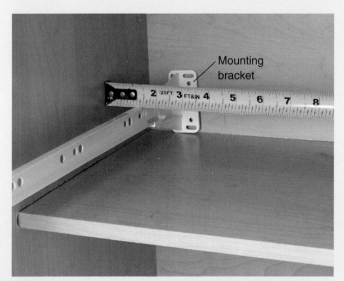

1 With the mounting bracket on the slide and resting on the cabinet shelf, level the bracket and mark the front edge. Note: for a pullout tray at the bottom of a cabinet, the rear bracket will rest on the cabinet floor.

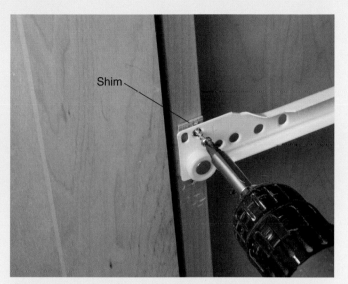

Shim

2 To attach the slide to the stile, drill pilot holes and drive two mounting screws. A shim was required here to allow the tray to clear the cabinet door. The shim was tacked on with a brad before the slide was attached.

Mounting bracket

3 Measure from the cabinet side to the slide at the front. Then adjust the position of the mounting bracket so that the slide is the same distance to the side at the back before screwing it to the cabinet back.

4 Attach the other half of each slide to the bottom edges of the tray, with the front (the nonroller end) of the slide flush with the front of the tray.

Glass-fronted drawers (left) make it faster to spot what you're looking for, especially if your closet has more than a few drawers. Drawer organizers (below left) help keep jewelry organized. Cabinetry may include a closet island (below), as well as wall and base cabinets that help keep your closet looking neat.

Drawers and Cabinets

I t may seem like Chinese boxes, but many closet designers like to include at least a few drawers and cabinets inside clothing closets. Although they add to the cost of reorganizing a closet, drawers are often better than shelves for storing small items. Organize them with dividers if necessary. Many closet system manufacturers make drawers with transparent fronts or in the form of wire mesh bins so that you can see what's inside without having to pull them open.

THE CASE FOR CABINETS

Cabinets are sometimes used in closets to store small personal items that might otherwise get swept or knocked off shelving easily. Cabinets enable you to store items you don't want in plain sight or that you don't want exposed to dust and light. Cabinet doors can be locked or childproofed as well.

Closet Fact: Italy is a leader in fashion and design, so it's no surprise the Italians make wonderful closets, too. The industry is concentrated in Northern Italy.

This custom closet, designed by architect Richard Wolf, was built after taking an inventory of the owners' clothing and accessories, which included a large collection of shoes, ties, and hatboxes. Maple was used throughout and left natural because the long, narrow space had limited natural light. Even the necktie rack and footstool (below) were made in matching maple.

Custom Closets

Custom is one of those words that gets overused, so sometimes it's difficult to know what it means. Some closet system manufacturers, for example, use the word to indicate that the components were cut at the factory to fit a specific closet. The components are not truly custom but customized. Their dimensions, and to some extent, hardware and finish change from closet to closet, but not much else is different.

True custom closets, however, are built from scratch, typically by a carpenter or cabinetmaker, exactly to your specifications. Choices of materials, hardware, components, and finishes are unlimited. This is usually, but not always, a more expensive and time-consuming approach to reorganizing a closet than installing a factory-made "custom" system. But the results may be worth it to you. If you want something that a closet company doesn't offer—a special wood or door material, for example—go the custom route. But be sure to do the necessary planning. While closet manufacturers typically help with design and installation as part of their services, for a custom job you'll have to hire your own designer and contractor. Above all, have detailed drawings and a contract that spells everything out before the work begins, or else you can expect changes, extra costs, and misunderstandings down the road.

Closet Doors: More Choices Than You'd Guess

One of the nice things about closets is that they hide clutter from view, so doors are usually desirable. Choosing the right door, however, is important for other reasons. It affects accessibility, lighting, ease of operation, traffic, room decor, and wall and space usage, as well as whether you can opt for back-of-door storage. Here's a rundown of some of your closet door options.

Sliding (or bypass). Sliding doors, also known as bypass doors, are the most popular solution for wide closets. Two or more panels hang and slide on tracks mounted at the top of the closet door opening. Sliding door panels can be paneled, flush, mirrored, or even made of clear, tinted, or frosted glass. The advantage to sliders is that they don't intrude upon the room, so you can position a chair or table nearby without fear that a swinging door will bump into it. The disadvantage is that you don't have full-width access to the closet contents. You can only get access to half the closet at a time.

Bifold. Bifold doors are a popular alternative to sliders for wide closets. They also work for more-narrow openings. The bifold panels can be wood paneled, mirrored, louvered (vented), or any one of a number of other styles. Bifold doors are pretty nifty in that they don't intrude far into the room (half as much as a swinging door), and they don't obstruct much of the closet opening either. Bifold door hardware is a bit fussier than the hardware for sliding doors, so expect them to need minor adjustments occasionally—but bifold doors are also a lot easier to remove if necessary, such as when you need to paint.

Hinged single. Hinged single doors are the most common solution for closets with small openings. The hinges can be on either side, or on both sides in the case of a split or double door. Hinged single doors have some negatives, though, including the infringement of living area, but there are some pluses, too. They are

Sliding doors, unlike hinged doors, do not swing into a room and infringe on available space or traffic. You can, however, get access to only half of the closet at a time.

Special bifold door hardware allows these doors to be swung back flat against the wall, permitting 100 percent access to this compact home office.

easier to lock. If you're storing valuables or toxic or hazardous items, this is important. They can also support a lot of weight, so you can use the back (or front) of the door for hanging mirrors, ironing boards, hanger arms, and a variety of over-the-door organizers.

Pocket and wall-mount. If you're remodeling, adding on, or building new, pocket doors are a time-honored way to have closet doors without causing traffic problems or losing space to swinging doors. (See photo on page 92.) The door slides into the wall cavity, all but disappearing from view. Pocket doors require an adjacent non-load-bearing area equal in width to the door plus several inches. Pocket door widths measure up to 60 inches. Two side-by-side pocket doors may also be used for larger openings.

Want a pocket door without having to tear open an existing wall to install it? Wall-mounted sliding doors are affixed to a track on the outside of a wall, above the door opening. (See page 149.) These doors require special wall-mount hardware and unobstructed wall space to one side of the opening.

French doors. French doors, typically hinged and double, offer a good-looking but more expensive closet door option. The glass allows more light into the closet than a solid door. With curtains, you can keep closet contents hidden. French doors fitted with mirrors instead of glass can make a room feel bigger. Negatives, besides cost, are the hazards that go with having glass in the home and the loss of floor space that must be reserved for opening any hinged door.

Door alternatives. Closets don't require doors. You can also run curtains, shades, or blinds across the opening or use a folding divider to hide closet contents from view. Dividers are freestanding and available in many materials, including paper, wood, wood shutters, mirrors, canvas, and other fabrics.

For a low-cost alternative to doors, use curtains to hide closet contents. Here, an old oar serves as the curtain rod. A wooden pole (called round stock) or standard curtain rods may be used as well.

For a closet like this one, the homeowner or a representative of the closet manufacturer takes the necessary measurements. Parts are then precut at a factory and delivered, with other components, for either homeowner or professional assembly.

Closet Systems

A great number of closet companies manufacture a variety of ready-to-assemble closet organizing systems. Each system includes a method of installation and its own menu of organizing components. Some systems are freestanding—they rest on the floor. Others are wall hung, either on a horizontal rail or directly attached to the wall. Organizing components include shelves, pullout bins, rods, racks, and more. While you can install many of these systems yourself, some systems are only available installed by professionals.

Closet systems are made from several types of materials. Common materials include laminated fiberboard and chrome-, vinyl-, or epoxy-powder-coated wire. (See "Not All Laminates Are Alike," on page 38.) Some companies make systems with solid wood shelving and components.

Many closet companies provide online design help, allowing you to use their software to plan a closet system yourself or with the help of one of their staff designers. Some companies will even send a designer to your home. Obviously, the cost (in one way or another) becomes greater the more design service you use. That said, there's no substitute for starting any project with a carefully thought-out design—and the people who do this every day are probably going to be very good at it.

Modular versus Non-Modular

There are two approaches to manufacturing closet organizing systems. One is modular and the other is not. With modular systems, the components can be arranged in a variety of configurations. The modules do not share sidewall dividers with other components. Non-modular systems, often called "custom" closets, are designed for a specific closet space. All of the pieces fit together like a puzzle. With a lot of thinking (and some sawing and drilling), you might be able to reconfigure a non-modular closet system, but it wouldn't be easy. Modular systems use more material, but offer more flexibility—including the benefit of being to take the system with you when should you move. Non-modular systems make somewhat better use of the closet space available to you, but they are considered permanent.

With non-modular construction (top), components share dividers (vertical panels), making it difficult to rearrange them. In modular construction (above), dividers are not shared.

FIBERBOARD AND WOOD SYSTEMS

Closet systems made of laminated fiberboard have the appearance of furniture. They include a variety of shelves, drawers, cabinets, and hardware components. Fiberboard systems are available in a large number of styles and colors, including faux wood finishes. With most fiberboard systems, vertical dividers carry the weight of stored items. Depending on which system you choose, dividers can be freestanding or hung on horizonal rails. (See "Install Fiberboard Closet Systems," on page 39.) They are predrilled for adjustable shelf supports. The dividers can accommodate clothing rods, cabinet doors, specialty shelving for shoes, and sliding hardware for various pullouts and drawers. Some useful pullouts include hampers, tie and belt racks, pants racks, packing shelves, and valet rods.

Smart Tip

The best way to learn about laminates and substrates is to look at samples. You'll be able to see laminate thickness, edge finish, and substrate material. These examples show particleboard (top) and medium-density fiberboard (MDF, bottom).

Not All Laminates Are Alike

There are many grades of substrates, laminates, and finishes used to make closet components, and sometimes it's difficult to tell one from another. Because they may affect performance, however, the grades are worth learning about before making a purchase.

Getting to know substrates. Fiberboard is the generic term for materials used to construct non-wire closet components. Several types are available:

• Particleboard consists of small wood chips and shavings bound together with resin. Used by most closet manufacturers, it comes in many grades, depending on how it's made, the chip source, and the resin.

• Medium-density fiberboard (MDF) consists of fine wood fibers bound together with resin. It is denser and smoother than particleboard, and it costs more . Both fiberboard and particleboard require special joint fasteners; screws and nails don't hold well and cause splitting.

• Hardboard, also called high-density fiberboard, is made by compressing exploded wood fibers into sheets. It is denser and stronger than MDF. Tempered hardboard is treated with linseed oil and baked to resist moisture. Hardboard is used for drawer bottoms and, when perforated, for wall-hung organizers.

• Plywood consists of wood layers glued together. The wood grain direction alternates with each layer. Plywood is available in many grades and wood species and is superior to fiberboard. It's more expensive, too.

Getting to know laminates. The most affordable option is usually a paper laminate. It comes in many colors and wood grains. Paper is glued and pressed to a substrate, usually particleboard or MDF, and coated with polyurethane. Both the grade of the paper and of the coating can vary, affecting appearance and performance. More-expensive coatings, for example, can simulate the tactile feel of real wood.

Melamine resin laminate, also known as low-pressure laminate, is a step up from paper laminate. Melamine resin is used to impregnate paper, which is bound to a substrate under 300 to 500 pounds per square inch (PSI) of pressure. Available in hundreds of colors and wood-simulating finishes, melamine is durable enough for most closet applications.

Three-dimensional (3-D) laminates, also known as rigid thermofoils (RTF), are rigid vinyl sheets that are sometimes used as laminates on closet system components. They come in many colors and wood grains, and they resist impact and staining well. The main advantage of RTF over paper and melamine laminates is that it conforms to complex shapes, such as a raised panel door, and is seamless (no need for edge banding).

Levels of quality vary significantly based upon the grade of the substrate and the type of surfacing or finish used on the components.

Wood systems are more expensive than fiberboard systems but offer some real advantages. There is no off-gassing of formaldehyde, a concern with fiberboard products. The shelves and dividers can be made with slats, improving air circulation. Solid wood shelving is less apt to sag. If damaged, wood is easier to repair than laminated fiberboard products, and unlike fiberboard, wood joints do not require special fasteners. Finally, solid wood components will stand up better to disassembly for moves.

Solid wood systems cost 30% to 40% more than fiberboard systems, but components will typically last longer and perform better.

How To: Install Fiberboard Closet Systems

About 15 years ago, fiberboard closet systems underwent something of a revolution. Instead of sitting on the closet floor, the components were hung on a steel rail, similar to the ones used by some manufacturers of kitchen cabinets. Although the former stacking types of closet systems are still available, rail-hung systems are easier to install. Problems related to uneven floors, baseboards, and cabinet stability (the possibility of cabinets toppling forward) are eliminated. And as a bonus, the units are off the floor for easier cleaning. All you'll need to install one of these rail-hung systems is a pencil, level, drill, and screwdriver.

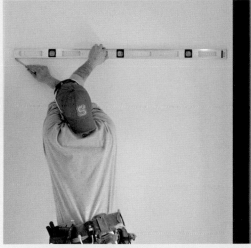

1 Mark stud locations. Then draw a level line to mark the location of the hanger rail.

2 Secure the rail to the wall with screws at studs and with wall fasteners where there are no studs.

3 Hang the dividers on the rail at the precut notches. (The notch is marked with an arrow.)

4 Attach the top shelf to the divider tops using the supplied joint fasteners.

5 Attach the remaining shelves and rods according to the manufacturer's instructions.

6 Ready to be loaded. Observe the manufacturer's shelf weight limits, especially on long shelves.

Saving MONEY

You can purchase wire systems piece by piece or as kits sized for standard closet dimensions. With the former approach, you can just buy what you need. Kits, however, cost less than if you were to buy the parts separately, so if the kit meets your needs, buying it will save you some money.

Wire shelving may be supported with poles and pole brackets (above and right) or diagonal braces (opposite). Use the former for heavy loads.

WIRE SYSTEMS

Wire closet systems are the least expensive of organizing systems. They are made from steel wire coated with vinyl or an epoxy powder finish and are readily available at hardware stores, home-improvement centers, and online. Epoxy coatings resist chipping and peeling better than vinyl coatings. Other finishes include chrome or zinc plating, and stainless steel. Such systems are relatively lightweight, easy to keep clean, efficient at using space, good at promoting visibility of stored items, and good at maintaining air circulation. They also stand up well to the moist conditions sometimes found in laundry rooms, basements, and garages. Wire shelving comes in several types, including linen, pantry, and fine mesh. Wire spacing can be ½ or 1 inch. Manufacturers also offer many accessories, including inclined shoe shelves, wire bin pullouts, and tie and belt racks.

Closet Fact: On a cold day in 1904, after being frustrated that there were not enough coat hooks at his workplace to hang his heavy coat—and tired of the coat becoming wrinkled when he laid it behind his chair—Albert J. Parkhouse bent some heavy wire into the first wire hanger. It enabled him to hang his coat just about anywhere.

How To: Install Direct-Mount Wire Systems

There are several ways to install wire shelving. The traditional approach is called "direct mount" because you fasten the diagonal shelf braces, rear shelf clips, and end-mounting brackets directly to the wall. The hardware and installation basics are shown below. A second approach uses both direct-mount hardware and poles onto which you attach shelf clips. (See the photos on the opposite page.) Shelving for direct-mount systems is not adjustable. For height-adjustable wire components, see "Install a Rail-and-Standard Wire System," on page 42.

1 Direct-mount wire shelving is supported by clips at the rear of the shelf and by diagonal braces along the front.

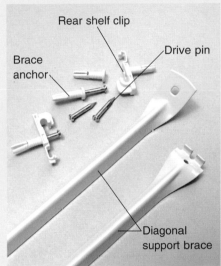

2 Bore ¼-in.-dia. holes through drywall for shelf and brace anchors according to the supplied template. Anchors work in drywall or wood.

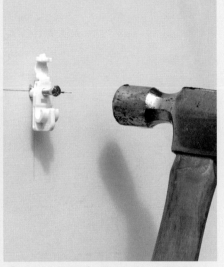

3 Insert shelf clip anchors in the holes. Then gently tap the drive pin through the clip to expand the anchor wings behind the drywall.

4 Insert the anchor through the foot of the brace. Then tap the drive pin into the anchor to expand the wings and secure the fastener.

5 Attach shelving to the support braces as shown. Then press the rear shelf bar into the rear shelf clips, and close the screw cover.

6 Direct-mount wire systems offer fewer accessories, but shoe shelves, easy-slide hanger rods, and pullout wire bins are available.

How To: Install a Rail-and-Standard Wire System

Just as hanger rails simplified the installation of fiberboard closet systems, so too have they made it easier to hang shelving standards. (See "Install Fiberboard Closet Systems," on page 39.) Best of all, these systems can carry enormous amounts of weight because the loads are transferred to studs—not just to drywall. Begin an installation of a rail-and-standard system by locating a stud. You may use an electronic stud finder, or you can repeatedly drive a small finishing nail into the drywall until you strike a stud. Then mark 16-inch intervals to locate the other studs. Or, even easier, you can rely on the spacing of the predrilled rail holes to locate subsequent studs.

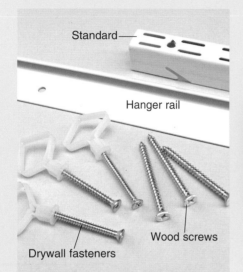

Standard

Hanger rail

Wood screws

Drywall fasteners

1 Hardware for rail-and-standard systems includes both wood screws and drywall fasteners.

2 Level and fasten the rail to studs using screws. When one hole aligns with a stud, others should, too.

3 Hang standards on the rail. The standards have a precut notch. Fasten the standards to the wall.

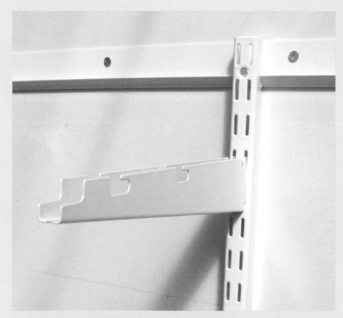

4 Install the shelf brackets by hooking them into the slotted standards. The brackets are designed to accept various attachments, including rod hangers.

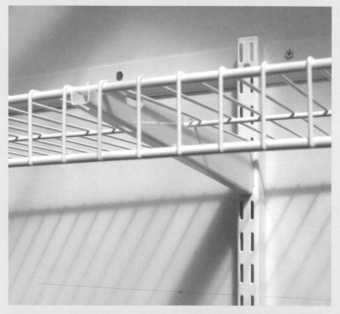

5 Snap shelving into the bracket slots. Be sure to purchase the correct bracket for the shelf length you desire. Deeper shelves require longer brackets.

RAIL-AND-STANDARD WIRE SYSTEMS

Rail-and-standard systems rely on wall studs for support. Typically, you hang the standards from a rail at 2-foot intervals. You can then insert shelf brackets in the standards' slots at the desired heights. Rod hangers, which are hook-shaped supports for closet rods, attach to the shelf brackets. You can then mount a variety of other components, including slide-out baskets, cubbies, and drawer towers, on the standards. Rail-and-standard systems often combine components made of differing materials. The shelves and drawers may be fiberboard, wire, or wood.

The wire shelves of the rail-and-standard closet above are trimmed with wood for a more finished, less utilitarian appearance. The system at right includes a mix of wire-mesh and fiberboard components.

Coat Closets and Mudrooms

Chapter 3

TYPICALLY LOCATED NEAR the front or back door, coat closets and mudrooms are often jam-packed with coats and jackets that are rarely used. They are also catchalls for sports equipment, footwear, umbrellas, and other odds and ends. Coats and jackets get tossed on chair backs or sofas. When people visit, their coats must be carried to a bedroom because there's no way to hang them by a door. You can change all that.

Multiple hooks accommodate family coats and jackets. When company is coming, make room by moving family outerwear elsewhere.

Smart Tip

Tracked-in grit can wear out floor finishes and carpeting. So it stands to reason that front and back doors are the places to set up your first lines of defense against dirt. Fiber mats outside the entry doors and carpeting inside will capture most of it. In winter, it's these same entry points that allow water, mud, and salt to enter. Place a large metal tray or rubber mat beside the door for wet footwear.

Winning Back Your Coat Closet

Win back your coat closets this winter by first removing coats and other items that you never or rarely use. If you can eliminate three winter coats, you can save a foot or more of space, enough to install a column of cubbies in which you can put gloves, scarves, and mittens. Find other places to store the infrequently used items you'd like to keep. In the spring, move winter coats to other storage spots, and make way for lighter jackets, sweaters, warm-weather sports equipment, and beach gear. The same goes for footwear. The boots of winter should give way to the sandals of summer. Don't try to store four seasons of outerwear and footwear in a coat closet!

It's impossible to keep shoes organized on the floor of a coat closet. Buy a shoe rack that's big enough for the most often used footwear, and place it near the entry door you use most. Store the rest on racks in the garage.

Don't Forget...

When designing a coat closet or mudroom, make a list of what it must store. Here are some suggestions to get you started.

- backpacks
- beach balls
- beach chairs
- beach towels
- beach toys
- board games
- boots
- broom
- canes
- cat litter
- coats
- coolers
- dog leashes
- dog toys
- duffle bags
- fans
- fire extinguisher
- first-aid kit
- flip-flops
- flying discs
- galoshes

- gardening tools
- gloves
- hats
- house flags
- insect repellant
- jackets
- kites
- laundry baskets
- luggage
- lunch/cooler bags
- mittens
- outerwear of guests/visitors
- pet food
- ponchos
- purses
- raincoats
- reusable grocery bags
- salt (for melting ice/snow)

- scarves
- shovels
- sleds
- slippers
- snow pants
- sports equipment
- step stools
- strollers
- sunglasses
- sunscreen
- swimming goggles
- tote bags
- towels (to dry off)
- toys
- travel bags
- umbrellas
- vacuum accessories
- vacuum cleaners
- water bottles
- wrapping paper

For a freestanding coat closet near the front entry, choose a more formal component. This one has a tougher-wearing laminate than that which you'd find on many bedroom closet organizers.

At the Front Door

The coat closet is the first thing visitors see when entering your home, so take some time to move what shouldn't be stored there and reorganize what should. Ideally, you should be left with enough room to hang the outerwear of at least a few guests.

In addition to coats, coat closets should be able to handle a host of small items, including gloves, mittens, and scarves in cold weather and sunscreen, insect repellants, sun hats, and the like in warm weather. (See the list above.) One solution is to install a small chest of drawers at one

Closet Fact: A popular cartoon, first appearing in movie shorts in the '50s and on TV in the '60s, depicted a near-sighted curmudgeon named Mr. Magoo. He got laughs by mistaking his over-stuffed closet for the front door. When he'd open it to leave the house, he'd get buried.

By lowering the rod height, you can add extra shelves at the top of a coat closet.

side of the coat closet for storing small items. Hang jackets or sweaters you're using regularly on a rod installed above the chest. Hang longer coats, such as rain slickers, to the side of the chest. Reserve the floor space below for boots. An alternative approach is to install a drawer tower. Put double-hang rods to one side and a single rod for longer coats to the other.

Another possibility is California Closets designer Lisa Lennard's favorite approach: measure your longest coat, and add 2 or 3 inches. Install a rod at this height. There should be room for two or three shelves above it, where you can put baskets or boxes for small items. If there's room for a double-pole arrangement beside the single pole, it can be used for hanging shorter jackets, and you'll still have room for a shoe rack below.

Back-of-door storage. Hinged single or double doors can be used to support a variety of organizers. You may use hooks for regularly used garments or over-the-door shoe organizers. Take care, however, not to overload this space, because hanging too much here will be unsightly and hinder access to the closet.

Saving MONEY

An inexpensive over-the-door organizer can be used for more than shoes. It can be used to store winter items, such as mittens, gloves, earmuffs, scarves, and knit caps. In summer, use it for sandals, water shoes, swimming goggles, sun block, small toys, and electronic games.

Options: Three Ways to Outfit a Mudroom

1 Hooks, bench, and board. In a household of two, a simple bench with storage below and a row of hooks is enough for a basic mudroom. Attach the coat hooks directly to a ⅜-inch plywood panel that's screwed to the wall studs in at least three places.

2 Fit for a foyer. A custom-crafted mudroom organizer combines a bench, hooks, and divided shelving. The bench has large drawers for easy access to under-seat boot and shoe storage.

3 Room for everyone. Individual baskets and bins allow each family member his or her own space. Coats and backpacks go in pullouts, and boots and shoes go in open compartments below the bench.

Mudroom organizers often need to dodge windows and wall switches. Fiberboard components do the job well but should be covered with melamine laminate to withstand mudroom rigors.

At the Back Door

Back-door closets, or mudrooms if you're lucky enough to have one, often serve a multitude of functions. In warm weather, they're host to cushions for outdoor furniture, toys, umbrellas, and small garden tools. In cool weather, it's boots, snow shovels, and ice scrapers. Year-round there are brooms, mops, vacuums, step stools, tools, and emergency supplies. If the mudroom doubles as a laundry, there are also laundry baskets, detergents, bleaches, and the like. During the school season, if there are young children in the house, there are book bags.

Reorganizing these spaces deserves careful planning to suit your individual needs. In general, however, choose open storage, including lots of wall pegs and hooks, cubbies, shoe racks, and shelves. You don't want to seal up wet or soiled items.

Saving MONEY

If space is tight in your mudroom closet, a bench can add storage—and seating. Sit on it while you take off your shoes, and then flip open the top and put your items inside. Instead of a flip-top opening, some benches have stationary tops with two or three cubby areas below the seat.

Mudrooms and corners near back doors end up becoming messy heaps (right) because places have not been designated, nor space allocated, for everything that has to go there. An easy and inexpensive reorganization (below) includes standard-mounted shelves, rods, and pullout bins. The cubby module is where the mail goes (sorted by recipient) until you get to it.

BEFORE

AFTER

A space-conserving pocket door (left) keeps mudroom messiness out of sight. If you lack the room, open mudroom storage (above) will do the job. This one was created with a rail-hung wire system.

Closet Fact: **A mudroom may see puddles from wet, snowy boots; however, that doesn't make it a "water closet," which is not a storage closet but rather a flush toilet. The term comes from the British English definition of a closet as a small private room. In this case, it was a room with running water.**

How To: Build Simple Modules for a Family Coat Closet

This coat closet was built into a small, cupboard-style closet. The goal was to provide accessible storage for the whole family and to hide messy-looking shoes and boots. Narrow, hinged doors (F) are used so as to not interfere with the entry door. Dimensions must be revised to suit your enclosure, but overall dimensions for this project are provided on the drawing.

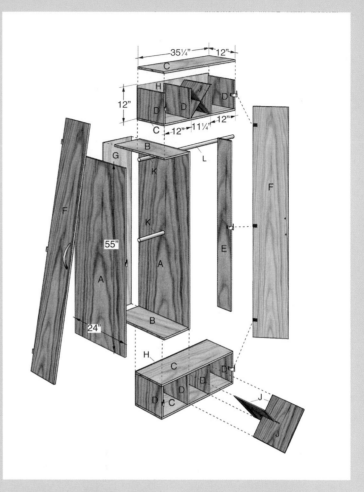

1 Assemble the three modules with ⅝-in. melamine boards or plywood. For this project, nails and glue may be used, but be sure to drill pilot holes prior to assembly to prevent splitting the fibers.

2 For strength, nail and glue ¼-in. backs (G and H) to each module. Insert the X-shaped dividers (J) into the cubby openings as shown.

3 Build a platform to raise the cubby module (parts C, D, and H) off the floor. It will make it easier to reach shoes stored behind the cubby.

4 Screw modules to the platform and the closet sides and top. Use clamps to hold modules in alignment and shims, if needed, to plumb them.

Half open and half closed, literally: this closet's doors hide the left and right thirds of the inside but not the center area. Leaving one section open allows users to quickly grab frequently used items, and the doors won't interfere with the entry door. Other features include child-height hanger rods and a compartment for hiding away footwear.

Making Room for Kids

Smart Tip

Kids don't like to put things away, so if you expect them to be neat, make it easy for them. In a coat closet, raise the pole and top shelf to make way for a second pole that they can reach. Better yet, install a rack of pegs or hooks below the top pole. Low hooks will keep kids from stretching to hang their belongings. Choose hardware that will hold backpacks and bulky jackets securely and that won't poke an eye if a child were to fall against it. Include shelves in the recesses at the sides of the closet, and place baskets on them, one for each child. Have them store their scarves, mittens, caps, and other small items there. Label the baskets so that everyone knows which one to pull off the shelf, and color-code all baskets, cubbies, and hooks for each child.

Foyer and mudroom floors often get wet, so it's wise to invest in durable moisture- and slip-resistant flooring. Avoid carpeting or hardwood that can stain or get moldy, and install linoleum, vinyl, ceramic, stone, rubber (shown) or concrete instead. Pick a dark color to hide the dirt.

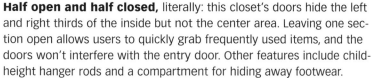

Kids' Closets

Chapter 4

ORGANIZING CLOSETS FOR CHILDREN is like buying growing kids sneakers. Do you buy a size bigger than is needed, so you're not back in the store next month, or do you aim for the perfect fit now, knowing you'll have to plunk down another $50 next month? Fortunately, with a carefully designed closet, you can have it both ways: a functional closet now and the basis upon which to reorganize and expand in the future.

If needed, you can reposition the rod and shelf heights as the child grows.

Children, once they can dress themselves, require convenient storage just like everyone else. Avoid situations like the one shown, and incorporate as much storage within reach as possible. A child's closet rod should be 42–48 in. from the floor. Use upper shelves for seasonal storage.

Closets That Grow with Your Child

Children go through several stages on the way to adulthood, and so do their closets. To meet their storage needs, you may need to reorganize their closets a couple of times before they can do it for themselves.

Fortunately, many closet organizing systems will allow you to do this without having to spend much additional money. Just be sure you purchase a system that makes it easy to adjust the heights of clothing rods and shelves and to add standard components, such as pullouts and shoe racks, as you need them. Any of the rail-hung systems, whether they be wire or fiberboard, will allow you to do this without much fuss.

YOUNG CHILDREN

With very young children, you're pretty much designing the closet to suit your needs, not theirs. Incorporate rods, doubling or even tripling them if necessary, for the current season's outfits. Pullout bins are handy for the week's supply of diapers, wipes, creams, powders, and related sundries. Use bins and boxes for blankets and sheets, sleepers and sleep sacks, T-shirts, socks, and the like. Reserve floor space for hampers and diaper pails.

Primary school-age kids. As kids get older, you'll want to get them in the habit of dressing themselves. Being self-sufficient in small ways now translates to being

Don't Forget...

When designing a child's closet, make a list of what it must store. Here are some suggestions to get you started.

- backpacks
- baseball cards
- bathrobes
- belts
- board games
- books
- casual shirts
- casual slacks
- CDs
- coats
- dolls
- dress shirts
- dress slacks
- dresses
- footwear
- electronic gadgets
- gloves
- hats
- jackets
- jeans
- jewelry
- luggage
- mittens
- musical instruments
- pajamas
- purses
- puzzles
- scarves
- school supplies
- skirts
- socks
- sports equipment
- stuffed animals
- sweaters
- swimsuits
- toys
- trophies
- T-shirts
- undershirts
- underwear
- video games

Shelving and rod lengths, as well as heights, can be adjusted should this closet need to be reconfigured as the child ages. The rods telescope, and the shelves nest, so they can be lengthened or shortened without cutting.

self-sufficient later. Young children don't usually have a lot of clothing that needs to go on hangers, so install mostly shelves and pullout bins in the bottom half of the closet. One short rod at about 42 inches should be sufficient for hung items the child will need to reach, such as jackets and bathrobes. Reserve floor space for bins in which toys and sports equipment can be stored.

Install more shelving and a rod or two for fancy clothing in the top half of the closet. For now, these will mostly be used by you to store your child's off-season and dressy clothing. In the future, however, your child will be able to put them to good use.

In closets for toddlers, pullout bins and pull-down boxes will help keep baby necessities in order. Many of the same components can be rearranged as the child ages.

Smart Tip

If you want kids to pick up their clothes, make it fun. Kid-friendly hangers are available shaped like animals, including one shaped like a monkey. One of the arms acts as the hook, and the legs act as the clothes hanger. You can also purchase hangers with officially licensed National Football League (NFL) and Major League Baseball (MLB) logos at some discount department stores.

Kids' hangers should be about 8–10 in. wide for infant clothing and 12–14 in. wide for children's sizes. These playful monkey hangers are made from fiberboard.

Storage cubes for kids can be configured for use as an open closet with a pole and shelf, as shown, or simply stacked in columns or pyramids for toy and clothing storage. They can be fitted with doors or left open as cubbies.

Closet designer Lisa Adams recommends including pull-down rods in a child's closet to maximize the space. Children will be able to pull them down themselves by age 5 or 6.

How To: Build a Child-Friendly Shoe Rack

Make putting away shoes fun, or at least almost fun, with this "boot" rack. On a sheet of kraft paper, draw a grid that's at least 6 columns by 11 rows. Space the lines 2 inches apart. Then trace the boot shape, one square at a time, according to the pattern below, right. This will be your template for the two rack supports.

Use scissors to cut the template from the kraft paper, and tape it to a piece of ¾-inch plywood. Trace the shape to the plywood. Then, using the wood as economically as possible, trace the template a second time.

Use a saber saw to cut out the two rack supports. Then bore ³⁄₁₆-inch-diameter holes 1 inch apart for boot laces; sand; and prime. Bore ½-inch-deep holes for the ¾-inch-diameter dowels. Cut six wooden dowels to 30-inch lengths, and assemble with glue.

Paint the rack supports using acrylic enamels; allow to dry; and glue the dowels into their holes (below). Now lace up the "boots," and pile on the shoes!

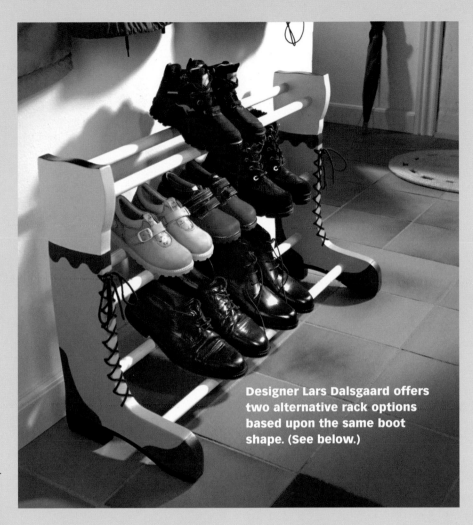

Designer Lars Dalsgaard offers two alternative rack options based upon the same boot shape. (See below.)

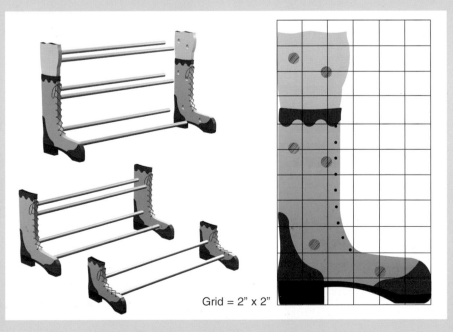

Grid = 2" x 2"

How To: Build a Steamer Trunk Wardrobe

Kids are small; their clothes are small—and so is their wardrobe. So why not give them a kid-size closet? This one, designed by Lars Dalsgaard, is shaped like a big steamer trunk. It fits in nearly any corner and frees up the room's adult-size closet for other things, such as toys.

Building the trunk. Construct the plywood box first, using ⅝-inch paint-grade plywood for the top, sides, and bottom, and ⅜-inch plywood for the front and back. Fasten joints with glue and 1¼-inch finishing nails. Use a saber saw or circular saw to cut the lid. Sand the surfaces, and round-over all edges with sandpaper. Prime and paint the outside. Apply two coats of varnish on the inside and along exposed edges.

Shelving can be supported with the shelving pegs and holes or with cleats. The rods are held in place with rod sockets. The rod in the lid is for hanging belts and ties. When you're done, begin collecting the travel stickers!

1 Construct a plywood box that measures 16 x 22 x 52 in. Nail and glue all joints. Then mark and saw off a lid that is 4 in. deep.

2 Paint the exterior a deep blue-green. Use masking tape and aluminum paint for the "metal" edges. Metal trunk corners add realism.

3 Add rods, a mirror, and shelving to the inside. Install four casters to the main part of the trunk and one to the outboard end of the door.

Shelves, bins, drawers, and triple and double closet rods help make the most of this closet space.

Older Kids' Closets

As children get older, their storage needs become similar to those of adults. Clothing becomes more important as kids become fashion conscious. There are still some differences to consider, however.

The preadolescent, aged 10 to 12 for girls and 10 to 13 for boys, is a great collector of stuff. Models, dolls, stuffed animals, sports cards, rocks and minerals, coins, stamps, and, for the investment-savvy youngster, action figures.

This closet design serves the needs of an older child through adulthood. The components will probably not need to be moved or modified.

Keeping It Neat

Admittedly, getting kids to pick up after themselves is a tall order. Address the problem in three ways. First, make it easier for them to find what they need. Kids always seem to have to be somewhere: soccer games, ballet lessons, school, and the like. If they can't find what they're searching for quickly, they tend to pull everything out until they find it—and then leave a mess on the floor. Incorporate many of the tips that improve visibility that have been suggested for adult closets, including lighting, pullouts, shallow shelves, rotating off-season items off-site, and so on.

Second, make it easier to put things away. Pullout shelves are easier than fixed shelves. Hooks are easier than hangers. Big bins are great for big items, such as balls and gloves.

Finally, include your kids in the closet-design discussions. If they feel that they have a say, they're also going to feel more obligated to keep things neat.

If your child feels that he needs a safe place to display models where his little sibling isn't going to smash them, accommodate the wish. You'll be rewarded with a neater child.

Then there's sports equipment: balls, bats, mitts, gloves, rackets, sticks, cleats, and helmets. All of it has to go somewhere. The mudroom or garage are, of course, options. (See chapters 3 and 9.) But bedroom closets are favored by many kids. For the smaller items, cubbies work well. For very small items, a basket or box that can fit in a cubby or on a shelf is the answer.

Larger items, such as shoes and sneakers, are better stored in large wire pullout bins into which you can see or in floor baskets, where the items are at least corralled. If you have the space, there are also rod-hung shelves made of canvas and wood or metal. Reserve whatever drawer space you will create for socks, underwear, and T-shirts. Install about 6 feet of closet rod to accommodate preadolescents' growing number of hangable garments.

Don't forget hooks and pegs. They're great for any age, but they are especially good for kids. Everything from clothing and backpacks to baseball mitts and soccer cleats can be hung up quickly—and be just as easy to grab at a moment's notice. Best of all, they're inexpensive. Put them on the wall, backs of doors, and the sidewalls of closets. Just be sure to choose hooks that won't hurt if a child falls against them. Hooks should curve back, toward the wall. Pegs should have large knobs at the end.

Pull-down rods. With older children, you can install pull-down hanger rods to get the most from the upper reaches of a closet. Closet designer Lisa Adams says, "Pull-down rods allow kids to store stuff up high but reach it from down low. Plus, if there's enough vertical space, you can triple-hang the goods."

A tween's closet has to accommodate so much more than clothing. There are board games, electronics, DVDs, toys, dolls, and the like. In the 12-year-old boy's room shown in the photos on this page, the designer's solution was two closets, one for clothes and one for everything else. Pullout shelves and bins serve as the organizers for everything from shoes and clothes to toys.

Closet Fact: Many children's stories involve the closet. In C.S. Lewis's *The Chronicles of Narnia: The Lion, the Witch and the Wardrobe,* three siblings enter a magical land through a wardrobe. In *There's a Nightmare in My Closet,* by Mercer Mayer, a young boy learns to confront his fears. And in the computer-animated film *Monsters, Inc.,* the monsters enter kids' bedrooms through closets. The ensuing screams are used to meet the power needs of Monstropolis.

This teen's dream closet has a place for just about everything, including clothes, craft supplies, toys, trophies, and other treasures. It even has a desk for doing homework.

TEEN CLOSETS

By the time a child becomes a teenager, he or she has not only been weighed down by years of getting gifts at birthdays and holidays but also has a whole new set of needs to accommodate. Expecting your teens to be neat without giving them some lessons in reorganizing will only lead to frustration for everyone.

Begin by encouraging your teenagers to give away clothing and other items they no longer use. For the things they want to keep, help them find alternative storage in the house, perhaps in an attic or basement. Of course, not everything from childhood needs to be stowed away. A prized collection of horse models or electric trains can go on shelving that runs the room perimeter near the ceiling. Stuffed animals can be clipped to a cord and hung from the ceiling or slung in a net that stretches from wall to wall.

Once your teen's possessions have been pared, introduce your child to the storage and organization principles explained in this book and elsewhere.

Teen storage action plan. Increase the amount of closet rod space by doubling up rods. Teens will need this because their collection of dresses, suits, and sports jackets will grow. Add shelving or pullout racks for shoes. Most teens prize their footwear and will have outgrown the idea of simply storing them in a basket. Add more shelving for handbags, sweaters, and sweats. Add drawers for personal items, such as music players, jewelry, and hair accessories.

Once your child has left the nest, the closet, such as this one (opposite), will be perfect for storing your off-season clothing, and you can leave some room for guests, as well.

Add inexpensive shoe shelves (above) to virtually any closet organizing system, including a freestanding unit.

Not enough closet space for your teen's needs? Install a free-standing closet (left), and fit it out with two rods, drawers, bins, and shelves.

Closet Fact: When Michelle Obama and her daughters, Malia and Sasha, visited First Lady Laura Bush at the White House in 2008, Obama and Bush discussed closets. Small wonder some discussion was necessary. The President's Bedroom, which traditionally serves as the master bedroom, has closets in the rounded north wall. The closet doors are papered and paneled to blend in with the rest of the wall.

Master-Suite Closets

PERHAPS THE MOST IMPORTANT closet in the house, the master-suite closet is where most homeowners begin and end every day. Its contents represent a significant investment made over a number of years. Moreover, garments and accessories are a personal expression of the owner, so they're special. Perhaps this is why, more than any other closet, the master closet needs to be not only functional but great-looking, too.

A reach-in closet such as this one can accommodate most of one person's wardrobe. Use dressers or secondary closets for the overflow, and store off-season clothing elsewhere to maximize the available space.

Dresser islands are a great way to use open space in a walk-in master suite. Besides the additional drawer space, the surface can be used for many tasks, including sorting, folding, ironing, and packing.

Smart Tip

Size shelves to the depth of what you're storing. In an adult's clothes closet, 14 inches is best because garments fold to about that depth. If the shelves are less deep, folded items will likely overhang the front edge of the shelf and look sloppy.

To Share or Not to Share

Whether or not you share the master closet with your soul mate has largely to do with how much closet space is available. The wardrobes of two people will typically need 16 to 20 feet of closet rod and 50 to 80 square feet of some combination of drawers and shelves. And this assumes you have a place to put seasonal clothing during its off season. If you don't have space for this much storage, even after paring down and moving nonessentials out of the bedroom, you have a few options.

Replace a dresser with a freestanding closet. (See the photograph on page 76.) These independent units make much better use of both the vertical space in a room and, thanks to numerous accessories, the closet space itself.

Move one person "off-site" but allow him or her (we're not going to say which) a rack of hooks in the bedroom to hang clothing currently in use as well a place for a bathrobe.

Expand the existing closet by taking space from an adjacent room or attic. Common strategies include taking down the wall between the master bedroom and an underutilized bedroom and using the space for a shared master bedroom closet and a new master bath. On the second level of many Capes and split-level homes, it's possible to grab space from an attic or over an eave.

A valet rod (right) pulls out to offer a place to hang items while making outfit selections or packing for a trip.

Swing-out and pullout racks (far right and below) give you a better look at slacks and ease removal.

A pullout pants rack (below) makes selection easy. A spiral rod (below right) does the same for items on hangers.

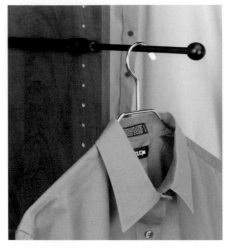

Will It All Fit?

When redesigning a closet, it's important to know how much space hung and stacked garments are going to use. Once you do, you can estimate how many feet of closet rod, how much shelving, and how many drawers you're going to need. Consult the tables at right and on the opposite page. Begin by counting the number of must-keep items you have for each listing in the first table. Divide it by the number in the center column. (Use the lower number for summer clothing and the higher for winter clothing.) Then add up the linear feet you'll need for garments of various lengths. You can, of course, group items with similar space requirements.

Width and Height Allowances for Hung Garments

ITEM SPACE	NUMBER THAT WILL FIT PER LINEAR FOOT	VERTICAL REQUIRED
Coats	4–5	38–60 in.
Shirts, blouses	12–15	27–45 in.
Pants	11–13	48 in.
Skirts	11–13	24–46 in.
Dresses	10	42–60 in.
Jackets	6	36–60 in.
Suits	6	54–60 in.

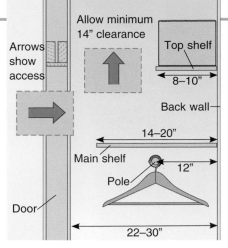

Add a second top shelf to a single-pole standard closet to increase storage. The pole height is 66–68 in. and is 12 in. from the back wall in such a closet.

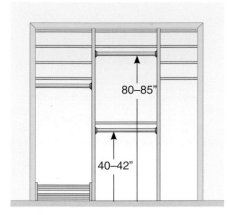

For double poles, install the top one 80–85 in. from the floor and the bottom one 40–42 in. from the floor.

Don't Forget...

When designing a master suite closet, make a list of what it must store. Here are some suggestions to get you started.

Men's Closet

- bathrobes
- belts
- boots
- briefcases
- casual shirts
- casual shoes
- casual slacks
- coats
- cuff links
- dress shirts
- dress shoes
- dress slacks
- exercise clothing/equipment
- gloves
- handkerchiefs
- hats
- jackets
- jeans
- jewelry
- luggage
- pajamas
- sandals
- scarves
- slippers
- sneakers
- socks
- suits
- suspenders
- sweaters
- swimsuits
- tie clips
- ties
- T-shirts
- tuxedos
- undershirts
- underwear
- watches

Women's Closet

- bathrobes
- belts
- blouses
- boots
- bras
- briefcases
- casual shirts
- casual shoes
- casual slacks
- coats
- dress shirts
- dress shoes
- dress slacks
- dresses
- exercise clothing/equipment
- gloves
- handkerchiefs
- hats
- hosiery
- jackets
- jeans
- jewelry
- lingerie
- luggage
- nightgowns
- pajamas
- purses
- sandals
- scarves
- skirts
- slippers
- slips
- sneakers
- socks
- sweaters
- swimsuits
- T-shirts
- underwear
- watches

DOES IT STACK UP?

When you stack clothing, pro organizers advise you to not go too high. It will make it tougher to retrieve a garment that's in the middle of the pile. Building a closet with a shelf every 6 inches, however, gets expensive. A good compromise is 12-inch spacing. So how many garments can you fit on a shelf? See the table at right, and make your estimate.

Closet Fact: According to a closet and storage study by Vance Research Services, the average size of the master closets built in 2008 was 49 square feet, and the average cost was $3,500.

Stack Heights for Piled Garments

ITEM	NUMBER THAT WILL FIT PER FOOT	HORIZONTAL SPACE REQ'D
T-shirts	14–16	10-12 in.
Shirts, blouses	8–15	12–14 in.
Pants	8–10	10–12 in.
Sweaters	4–6	12–14 in.
Blue jeans	8–10	10–12 in.
Shorts	10-14	10–12 in.
Boxers	12-14	8–10 in.

Smart Tip

Good shoes are expensive. Keep them looking good longer by using paper stuffing or wooden forms to maintain shoe shape. Polish them regularly. You may also choose to store shoes in their original boxes or in lidded plastic bins. Label the containers so you can find the pair you want quickly.

Wire rails keep shoes from sliding off shelves and allow you to see them.

A rotating shoe tree is a great way to use the corner of a walk-in closet.

Cubbies keep shoes and boots in order but are tougher to clean than shelves.

A pullout shoe rack mounts to the side of a divider and conserves space.

Fitting in the Rest

Shoes and accessories may require some math to be certain you're going to be able to fit everything in your new closet, but it's quite simple. Socks fit well in shallow drawers. They require about 9 square inches each. An average drawer has about 300 square inches and will nicely accommodate 30 pairs of socks. This number works for panty hose, bras, and panties, too.

Shoes require 10- to 14-inch-deep shelves, depending on shoe size. One pair takes up about 10 inches for men and 8 inches for women. Sneakers and boots are wider than shoes, but on average these numbers should work. A boot shelf will need extra height.

Belts and ties are best hung at eye level rather than winding them up and stuffing them into a drawer. It's easier to see them and to put them away, too. Handbags and hats can take up a square foot or more each. Allow enough shelving to accommodate them. Jewelry is best stored in lined and divided drawers designed for the purpose.

Closet Fact: According to a recent survey, women, on average, own 19 pairs of shoes. One in six has more than 30 pairs.

Controlling and Preventing Clothes Moths

I t's frustrating to pull a favorite sweater out of your closet only to find that a clothes moth has had it for dinner. More accurately, it was a moth larva—shiny, cream-colored, and not more than ½ inch long—that was the culprit. Larvae molt many times while making their journey to adulthood (when they, too, can lay eggs and begin the cycle all over again). During this time, they require nutrition. Wool, fur, hair, leather, carpeting, upholstery, and feathers can provide it.

Spotting an infestation. Adult clothing moths are small, reclusive, and short-lived. Not to be confused with food- and grain-infesting moths, they are weak flyers and quite small, only ¼ inch long with a ½-inch wingspan. Look for them in dark cracks and crevices or, better yet, use a clothes-moth trap to monitor whether you have an infestation (as well as to control it). Note: clothes-moth traps attract the most common type of clothes moth (the webbing clothes moth) but not other species, including the casemaking clothes moth. And don't expect a food-moth trap to lure and catch any type of clothes moth. The pheromones (sexual attractants) are different for each species.

Clothes-moth eggs and larvae are, of course, even smaller and harder to see than the adult moths. You'll know you have them if you spot the silky webbing produced by webbing clothes moths or the cocoonlike pupal case produced by the casemaking clothes moth. Larval casings, left behind after molting, may also be evident. A good flashlight and a magnifying glass will come in handy if you go searching.

Taking action. If you have an infestation, kill the larvae and eggs by laundering your wool garments in hot water for 30 minutes. If the garments cannot be washed in hot water, dry cleaning will do the trick. Less-easy methods for ridding clothing of clothing moths include cooling clothing to below 18°F. Put dry ice in a large cooler chest along with the affected clothing. Or put clothing outside on a cold winter day!

Insecticides work too but are less desirable for obvious health reasons, and they may stain your clothing. If you go this route, try a Pyrethrin-based insecticide spray. It does not leave persistent toxic residues, but you'll have to test the product for staining on an in-

conspicuous area of the garment before using. For persistant infestations, it may be necessary to call in a professional exterminator to solve the problem.

Prevention. To help prevent future infestations, clean your woolen garments regularly. Moths are more likely to feast upon fabrics stained by foods, perspiration, and the oils from your hair. Even hanging your woolen garments in the sun periodically and brushing them will remove the light-averse larvae and destroy eggs.

Mothballs, flakes, and crystals that contain naphthalene or paradichlorobenzene have been used for generations to protect clothing in storage. They are not a good choice in most homes because of their toxicity. (They must be kept away from children and pets.) If you do use mothballs, do not allow them to contact plastic, including buttons, hangers, and garment bags, because they can melt it. In addition, only use mothballs in airtight containers. Otherwise, the toxic vapors will not reach high enough concentrations to be effective.

Cedar closets and chests are of limited value. While the essential oils of eastern red cedar will deter some larvae, the cedar will lose its ability to repel the insects after a couple of years. A better storage solution is airtight containers. Avoid storing woolen garments in closets where high humidity is a problem.

Regular vacuuming in closets, under beds and other pieces of heavy furniture, behind radiators, along baseboards, and in other recesses will help prevent infestations, too.

It's the larvae of webbing and casemaking clothes moths that ingest natural fibers and cause damage to wool, such as this hole in the author's favorite cashmere sweater.

Options: Four Low-Cost Ways to Add Bins and Drawers

As previously mentioned, pullouts, whether they be shelves, trays, or racks, are key to easy-access storage. Drawers and bins are no exceptions. They are great places to store small items—such as stockings, socks, and panty hose—that might otherwise fall off shelving. If you don't want to spend $30 or $40 per pullout component, however, simple baskets and cardboard boxes work nearly as well. Just slide them on a shelf, and apply labels that identify contents if necessary.

2 Standard drawer kits can be hung from rails (as shown) or installed between the dividers of fiberboard organizing systems.

3 Special brackets, supported by vertical standards, accept the sliding frames shown above. Cloth bins of varying depths hang from the frames.

1 This tower of pullout bins is a low-cost alternative to a tower of drawers. As a bonus, the mesh construction allows you to see contents.

4 Plastic trays, divided for small items such as jewelry, can slide on and off shelves as needed. Decorative baskets and boxes can be used the same way.

Wire organizing systems make the best use of space. Very little volume is wasted on the components.

Smart Tip

Clothing stores are a good place to look for clues to smart clothing organization. Typically, hung items are below eye level, making clothing easier to see. Piles are shallow. Cubbies and dividers are prominent in high-end stores. Curved racks and rotating racks make good use of tight spaces. Lighting is bright without causing shadows.

Reach-in Closets

Reach-in bedroom closets are what most people own. They typically measure 8 feet tall, 6 feet wide, and 2 feet deep. The nice thing about reach-ins is that they don't waste floor space. The not-so-nice thing is that there's rarely enough room for two people's needs.

SHARED REACH-INS

Shared reach-ins are usually divided in right and left halves, so partners can get access to storage without bumping into each other. Generally, they are used only for hanging items because of space constraints. Items that can be folded or stacked may have to be stored elsewhere, such as in dressers or in a secondary closet. Choose bifold or pocket doors or a soft solution, such as curtains, when you must share a reach-in closet.

Saving MONEY

Wire organizing systems are not only less expensive than laminate systems, they also utilize the available space more efficiently. For example, the dividers and shelves in a typical bedroom closet, stacked together, would have a volume of about 4 to 5 cubic feet. Volume consumed by wire shelving is much less.

Pullout belt racks are easy to install and keep your belt collection at hand.

Laundry sacks hang on rods that pivot forward. When laundry day arrives, just grab the handles and go.

An extra-wide reach-in can store nearly all of a single person's wardrobe. Translucent closet sliding doors fit seamlessly with the pattern of the adjacent storage wall when closed.

These options will allow access to most of the closet when opened. Sliding doors are a real nuisance when two people share a reach-in closet and try to dress at the same time.

SEPARATE REACH-INS

Properly organized, the average-size reach-in closet is adequate for storing most of one adult's wardrobe. If a couple has two in their bedroom, each person gets one. The nice thing about separate closets is that it allows the storage to be tailored to individual needs. Adjust rod and shelf heights to suit height differences. Size storage components to accommodate differences in garment size, the number of shoes to be stored, and specific items, such as ties, scarves, and bras. A woman's reach-in closet, for example, can accommodate the greater variety of garment types often found in a woman's wardrobe. In addition to jeans, blouses, and T-shirts, there are fancy three-quarter-length tops and sweaters, wide belts, lingerie, handbags, and boots. Reserve a rod for long dresses and evening gowns. A man's reach-in may eschew the single rod to include more double-hang rods for sports jackets and suits.

Separate reach-in closets can also accommodate components with drawers and shelves, providing places for items such as wristwatches, jewelry, hosiery, and lingerie.

When trying to fit most or all of your wardrobe in an average-size reach-in closet, you will need to conserve space as much as possible. Remove items that can be stored elsewhere, such as extra bedding and hampers. Rotate seasonal clothing to secondary closets to prevent your closet from becoming overfilled.

Think Universal and Accessible

E ven if there is no one in your home with special needs, it's wise to think in terms of universal design—making homes appropriate for people with a wide range of abilities and disabilities. The Center for Universal Design recommends that 50 percent of all storage be less than 54 inches high. It also suggests height-adjustable closet rods and shelves, as well as power-operated carousels, to bring items within reach.

For a closet to be accessible to the physically challenged, there needs to be an opening large enough to accommodate a wheelchair, no raised threshold, and an accessible or automatic switch for lighting. There must also be a clear floor area that permits the forward or parallel approach of a wheelchair. In the case of the former, the ability to reach an item ranges from 15 to 48 inches. When parallel (or reaching from the side), the range is somewhat greater: 9 to 54 inches. Closet rods should be a maximum of 54 inches high.

Cabinet doors should have U-shaped pulls, as shown at left, or be touch-activated. Avoid pulls that require twisting or pinching hand movements.

Smart Tip

A garment with sleeves, such as a shirt or jacket, measures 22–24 inches from elbow to elbow. This means that the closet rod should be installed 12 inches from the back wall—or else the garment sleeve will press against the wall. It also means a reach-in clothing closet should be at least 24 inches from the inside door surface to the back wall.

Closet Fact: Between 1908 and 1940, Sears Roebuck and Company sold and shipped via rail more than 70,000 house kits, complete with studs and joists, drywall (or lath and plaster), shingles, nails, and paint—over 30,000 parts in all. Closets were included in the package. The Sears mail-order catalog boasted that its No. 9266 triple-unit clothes closet was "the best closet arrangement known in architecture."

Separate freestanding closets are an alternative to reach-in types when space is tight. A step stool makes access to top shelves easier.

Storing Hats

Many hats made from felt, straw, or other stiff materials require a fair amount of space for proper storage, and the hats often go for long intervals without being worn. A good place for them is a high shelf. Hatboxes are available for keeping fancy hats protected from dust. Just be sure to label the box so that you won't need to rummage when you need one. Caps can be stored on shelves or on straps fitted with clips. The straps stretch from the top of the closet door to its bottom. Soft fabric hats can be stored in a basket and placed on a shelf.

Use hatboxes to store items other than hats, too, including hair ribbons and hair accessories, dolls, and sunglasses. They can be had in any color and in several sizes. See sarahshatboxes.com for a wide selection.

Smart Tip

If you've used the available closet space as efficiently as possible and you still don't have room for everything, consider using the space under your bed. Lots of roll-out organizers are available, but the solution I like best is a platform bed with built-in drawers or a hinged mattress board that lifts up. The stored items stay dust free.

For a European look, in which the components seem to float, support rails are hidden behind ¾-in. panels. These panels are less than 1 in. from the wall, so little space is lost.

Walk-in Closets

Walk-in closets open up a world of possibilities: your entire wardrobe all in one space, a dressing area so that you don't have to carry clothing into the bathroom, and even a lounge chair where you can relax or read while your spouse is sleeping! Some designers consider walk-in closets the new room—a showcase that gets nearly as much attention as the kitchen.

Some walk-in accessories that would take up too much space in the average reach-in closet include a dressing table and chair, pullout packing table, mirror, television, computer, stereo equipment, ironing board, hamper, and bathroom scale. Cabinets can be used to hide clutter or, if they're glass fronted, to display personal photos or collections. For athletes, a walk-in closet provides a great place to consolidate gear and sports garments.

SHARED WALK-INS

Typically, a walk-in closet is a shared space of 48 to 64 square feet. It can, of course, be divided in many ways, including down the middle. In such cases, the minimum aisle should be wide enough to accommodate two occupants passing one another at the same time, or about 4 feet. If you're contemplating a dressing area, you'll need an additional area that's at least 20 square feet.

AFTER

The poorly used space in the walk-in closet below was transformed into the well-designed corner at left. Closely spaced (and easily adjustable) shelves keep folded items organized and help prevent the wrinkles that form when clothing is stacked high. Double poles make the most of the rod space. Deep shelving is ideal for storing bedding.

BEFORE

SEPARATE HIS AND HERS

If you have space to spare, separate walk-in closets are the ultimate in storage luxury. They are typically 35 to 45 square feet in area with at least a 3-foot-wide aisle.

Building separate closets adds significantly to construction expenses, including extra lighting, ductwork for HVAC, and framing. Benefits include having enough storage for your entire wardrobe, clothing accessories, and personal items in one place—and storage for bed linens as well.

This "hers" walk-in closet, built largely with wire components, measures 5 x 8 ft. and costs much less than the other systems here.

Leave an open shelf in a walk-in master suite closet that you can personalize with photos, sculptures, found objects, small lamps, and other favorite things.

Closet Fact: In 2008, Warner Bros. released an app for the iPhone or iPod touch called "Carrie's Closet," which allows users to photograph and share their wardrobe with others. You can use it to take inventory—or to plan the perfect outfit. The inspiration for the sotware is fashion icon Carrie Bradshaw, a character in *Sex and the City* who has clothes, shoes, and accessories that make her the envy of many women.

This spacious walk-in closet, designed by Shane Shupe of Rubbermaid, is tailored to the needs of a typical couple. The woman has a single rod to hang long garments and gets extra shoe-storage space. The man makes the most of double rods for sports coats and slacks.

Save Space with a Closet Carousel

Tired of a closet pole so jammed with garments that it's a struggle to hang something up or pull something down? Consider maximizing your closet space by hanging items on a circular or oval rotating track. Several companies offer "closet carousels," motorized conveyors that run on 110-volt power and rotate 360 degrees in either direction. Clothes hang in slots along the length of the conveyor. With the push of a button, the carousel rotates along the track, creating extra storage space and bringing your clothes and accessories to you.

Access is a breeze. So is setup. It shouldn't take the average homeowner more than a few hours to complete the assembly. No special tools are required. Once assembled, the height can be adjusted, and a number of accessories are available, including garment rods, baskets, storage trays, and shoe racks.

A closet as small as 6 feet wide by 4½ feet deep can have 20 linear feet of hanging space with a closet carousel, and the carousel can support about 140 pounds. A large carousel can provide 28 linear feet in an 8-foot space, and its weight capacity is approximately 190 pounds. Closet carousels are ideal for walk-in closets, but they can also be used in reach-in closets and pantry closets. Carousel systems can be custom designed to meet your needs. They can also go with you should you move.

Closet carousels can set you back about $2,000 to $3,500. If that's too much, consider a nonmotorized revolving stand, similar to units found in clothing stores. They don't have the same weight capacity, but then again, they cost only $130. See the Revolving Round Hang Bar Garment Rack from Fixturepronto at fixture-pronto.com.

A closet carousel is quiet, too—the machinery isn't much louder than an oscillating fan.

Off-Season Clothing Storage

Garments such as sweaters and swimsuits are often not used for half the year or more, so if your closets are cramped, it makes sense to move these items elsewhere. One possibility is under beds. You can build an under-the-bed storage unit, or you can buy lidded plastic bins that are shallow enough to fit under the average bed. Shallow baskets or even cardboard boxes will also work.

Storing off-season garments in a spare closet is another possibility. Zippered hanger bags keep the items dust free. "Space bags" use vacuum pressure to compress items in an airtight bag. Manufacturers claim you can reduce clothing or bedding volume by half or more. Many users report success, while others say that the seal does not last and the bags tend to inflate somewhat over time.

Closet Fact: Small apartments may only have a hall closet and a bedroom closet; some don't have any. According to the *New York Post*, some New Yorkers living in cramped apartments store their clothes in ovens, refrigerators, and kitchen cabinets because space is so tight.

This guest room closet includes drawers, rods, and shelves for garments, and it offers visitors ample floor space. Reserve some of the closet space for an extra set of bed linens and personal items you might find in a nice hotel room.

Create a Guest Closet

Most of us don't have the room to devote both a closet and a dresser to the occasional guest. You can, however, offer visitors a bit of storage of their own by installing rods, shelves, and drawers in a spare closet. Designate at least two drawers and one rod to guests. Leave floor space clear for luggage and footwear. To make your guests feel at home, stock the closet with hangers, towels and washcloths, a clothes iron, extra blankets or comforters, a hair dryer, paper, pens, and tissues. On the back of a cabinet or closet door, include directions for logging onto your wireless network. Use the remaining space for off-season storage, spare bedding, or overflow from your own closets.

Saving MONEY

Sliding doors can be a pain, especially on a shared closet. You can opt for bifold doors instead, but you'll pay for new doors, hardware, and paint. A less expensive option, assuming your old sliders aren't too wide, is to hang the sliders on hinges. Fit the old doors with knobs, and add bullet catches at the top. Hinged doors will allow you to hang mirrors and over-the-door organizers on either side of either door.

Linen Closets

Chapter 6

THERE ARE THREE KINDS OF LINENS that require storage in the typical home: table, bed, and bath. Rarely are table linens stored with bed or bath linens because kitchens and dining areas are usually some distance from bedrooms and bathrooms. Bed and bath linens are, however, frequently stored together. Bedroom closets can be good locations, but if you don't have the space, a central hallway closet works fine.

Linens are often stored in a hallway closet, such as this one with space-saving sliding doors. The linens-plus closet (opposite) stores bathroom supplies in addition to towels.

Antique Linens

Antique table linens often discolor while in storage, especially if stored on ordinary paper, metal, or unsealed wood. Prevent this by placing them on shelves lined with acid-free muslin or tissue paper. Use acid-free tissue paper to separate antique linens as well. Reduce creasing by hanging large linens on rods or with hangers that are not made from wire.

Table Linens

Dinner linen closets consist primarily of deep shelves spaced about a foot apart. Wire organizers mounted on vertical standards work especially well and allow the use of handy accessories, including shelf hooks and dividers. Wood or fiberboard shelves, lined with shelf paper, can also be used.

Use appropriately sized containers, such as canvas bins or baskets, to store sets of napkins, placemats, and table runners. You may want to consider storing candles, candle holders, and vases with your table linens so that they will be readily available after you spread the tablecloth.

Dish towels and pot holders are better stored in kitchen drawers so that they can be quickly grabbed as you need them. Aprons can hang behind a door or go in a drawer.

Short rods are often used in linen closets for hanging tablecloths. Doing so is especially sensible if you send fine linens out for laundering and they're returned on hangers.

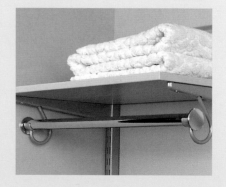

Smart Tip

Fold towels neatly and compactly for easiest storage on linen closet shelves. Typically, the best way to fold a towel is in thirds lengthwise and then into a rectangle. You can also fold them in thirds lengthwise, and then roll them for storage where space is limited. Rolling the towels will compress them and take up less space.

When reorganizing a linen closet, install 16-in.-deep shelves (left). If necessary, use 12-in. shelves at the top to ensure access to space behind the header.

Bed and Bath Linens

Closets for linens may serve several bedrooms and bathrooms. Often located in a central hallway, they may be used to store your towels, washcloths, sheets, pillowcases, extra pillows, comforters, and blankets.

As seen in the previous chapter, some bedding can be stored in the room in which it's used. But that strategy will probably not work for every bedroom. In some, there simply isn't enough storage space, and having to enter the master suite to get a pillowcase for the guest-room bed is not ideal. In such cases, a hallway linen closet may be used.

Sometimes linen closets are located in the bathroom. This is a less-than-ideal situation because linens should be stored in cool, dry places. You can make the best of it by ensuring good ventilation and limiting such closets to storing only the towels and washcloths you'll use in a week or two. In the remaining space, store bathing essentials, such as shampoos, body wash, and conditioners, and toiletry supplies, including extra rolls of toilet paper and soaps.

Closet Fact: Cabinets for linens, called "linen presses," were popular from the seventeenth to the nineteenth century.

No room in your linen closet for bulky items, such as blankets and comforters? Roll them up and stow them over the door to a spare bedroom.

Don't Forget...

When designing a linen closet, make a list of what it must store. Here are some suggestions to get you started.

- air fresheners
- aprons
- bath mats
- bath rugs
- bath towels
- bathroom scales
- beach towels
- bed skirts
- blankets
- candle holders
- candles
- cleaning supplies
- colognes
- comforters
- cosmetic bags
- coverlets
- curling irons
- curtains
- diapers
- dish towels
- doilies
- drapes

- duvet covers
- garbage bags
- garment bags
- hair dryers
- hair-care products
- hand towels
- hygiene products
- ice bags
- ice packs
- ironing boards
- irons
- laundry bags
- lightbulbs
- loofahs
- medical supplies
- medicines
- mirrors
- napkins
- oven mitts
- perfumes
- pillowcases
- pillows

- placemats
- pot holders
- potpourris
- quilts
- shades
- sheets
- shower curtains
- skin-care products
- slipcovers
- soaps (liquid/bar)
- sponges
- sprays
- step stools
- table runners
- tablecloths
- throws
- tissues
- toilet paper
- towels
- valances
- vases
- washcloths

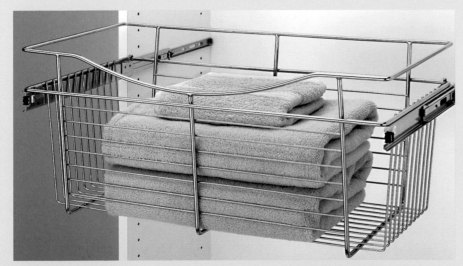

Large wire baskets keep towels orderly. Each one can store a full matching set.

Smart Tip

Top sheets, fitted (or contour) sheets, and pillowcases often become shuffled, making it difficult to find what you need. A good way to keep matching top sheets, contour sheets, and pillowcases together is to store them in a pillowcase.

Hallway or bathroom closets may be used to store linens. These large built-in units were designed to fit under a sloped ceiling. Oversize doors were cut to suit. See inset at the top of the opposite page.

A chifforobe with glass doors (right) is a stylish way to store bed linens, especially prized quilts. The compartment with the rod is for hanging pressed table linens.

HALLWAY LINEN CLOSETS

Hallway linen closets should be cool and dry. Wire shelving promotes air circulation, doesn't hold moisture, and is your least expensive option. Melamine laminate or slatted wood shelving works fine, too. When using wire shelving, choose the fine mesh variety. Small items, such as shampoo bottles, won't topple. Bins and baskets of various sizes can be added to help ensure that towels and sheets go back to their proper place. You can even label them, if you like, to remind family members about what goes where.

You will need as least three 16- or 18-inch-deep shelves. Install them in the lower half of the closet. The depths of the remaining shelves may decrease as they ascend, with the top shelf being 12 inches deep. In this way, you'll have better visibility of lower shelves. Smaller items can be stored on the higher shelves.

Smart Tip

Follow the "one in, one-out" rule. Many of us hesitate to get rid of old sheets and towels, which is a major cause of linen-closet congestion. When it's time to buy a new set of bed sheets or bath towels, remove a worn set, and tear them up for use as rags. (By the way, this rule works well for the contents of any closet!)

A linen wardrobe can store more than next week's linens. Here, cloth baskets keep lotions, creams, and a hair dryer that would otherwise clutter up the nearby vanity.

Ways to Keep Linens Fresh

No one enjoys coming out of the shower to a musty-smelling towel. The best way to avoid this is to promote good air circulation in the linen closet. Wire shelving and louvered doors help.

Some other tricks:

• Use odor absorbers. An open box of baking soda, placed at the back of the linen closet, is a good one. Some people place dryer sheets between linens.

• Linen sprays and herbal sachets also help to neutralize odors.

• Avoid placing clean linens on unfinished wood shelves. Paint the shelves, or line them with shelf liners.

• Never store towels or other linens while they're still damp.

• Limit the number of bedding and towel sets you store in the linen closet. A good number is what you will use in one month. When reaching for a new set, try to use those that have been stored the longest. If linens at the bottom of the pile go for long periods of time without being used, they will become stale.

Closet Fact: Few fabrics today are made of linen (example at right), a durable fabric woven from the fibers of the flax plant. (The Latin term for flax is *linum*.) Linen originally referred to a cloth made from this plant, but over time *linens* became the generic term for sheets, towels, napkins, and other goods made of cotton and other fibers. The earliest linens date back at least 12,000 years.

Kitchen Pantries

Chapter 7

IN CENTURIES PAST, the pantry was a room where food was stored and prepared. Silverware was also counted and kept there, watched over by a butler who often had to make the pantry his sleeping quarters (hence the phrase "butler's pantry"). The pantry all but disappeared from kitchens in the mid-twentieth century but has made a comeback in the last decade. Today a pantry can be a walk-in, reach-in, or pullout affair.

The reach-in pantry (left) keeps an assortment of drinks, foods, and paper products close to the food-prep area. Back-of-door shelving improves visibility and accessibility for small items. The pantry closet (above) combines wire shelving and fiberboard components on a rail-and-standard system. It has enough room to store pet food, large cookware, wine and beverages, root vegetables, and even a small kitchen cart.

Walk-in, Reach-in, and Cabinet Pantries

Not every food you purchase at the supermarket needs refrigeration. Some items, including onions and potatoes, require cool—not cold—storage. There are several ways to do it, depending upon the available space.

WALK-IN PANTRIES

If you've got 30 square feet or more, an unheated walk-in pantry off the kitchen is a great way to store a large volume of such items. You'll save valuable cabinet space at the same time.

Access to a walk-in pantry should be as close to the refrigerator as possible so that you can gather ingredients without affecting the food-prep area or cleanup zone. The north side of the house is usually coolest, so if you can put the pantry there, do so. Be sure it's well ventilated and well insulated to keep it from getting too warm during the

Closet Fact: The most famous pantry in literature belongs to Tom Sawyer's Aunt Polly. As every school child knows, Tom got caught taking jam from the pantry and then fled, eluding punishment.

A walk-in pantry with wooden shelves (left) has a finished look that matches nearby kitchen cabinetry better than an all-wire system. The setup of this pantry cabinet (above) offers pull-out wire baskets and wooden bins. Keep smaller items in the baskets where you can easily see them. Put large, heavy items, such as cookware, in the bins.

day. Root vegetables, such as potatoes and onions, will last longer in a cool, dark, dry pantry than they would in a refrigerator, but you aren't limited to root vegetables, of course. A walk-in pantry is a great place for canned goods, cereal, pasta, drink mixes, cookies, pet food, paper goods, and even appliances that don't get used every day. (See "Don't Forget..." on the opposite page.)

REACH-IN PANTRIES

The reach-in pantry is a space-saving option to the walk-in pantry. It can be installed in a closet or recess as shallow as 10 inches. Like walk-ins, it's best if reach-in pantries are away from heat sources and busy areas within the kitchen. Reach-in pantries are commonly outfitted with wire shelving. Fiberboard and wood components, though

more expensive, are also used, especially if the pantry is in view from the dining area.

Walk-in and reach-in pantries are good ways to add cool storage if you have the space, but most people do not. If you don't—or if you aren't planning to incorporate one into a remodeling—a base cabinet can act as a pantry, and there are freestanding pantry cabinets available, too.

PANTRY IN A CABINET

Many kitchens end up with narrow, leftover spaces at the end of cabinet runs. Such spaces are typically fitted with narrow cabinets and vertical dividers for storing such items as cookie sheets and cutting boards. They can also accommodate pullout pantries. A pullout pantry is basically a tall, narrow drawer (usually 9 to 15 inches wide) with

This newly built, well-lighted pantry is ready for stocking. About 30 square feet, it contains more than 80 linear feet of fixed shelves.

Don't Forget...

When designing a pantry, make a list of what it must store. Here are some suggestions to get you started.

- aluminum foil
- baking dishes
- beverages
- bowls
- candies
- canned goods
- cereal
- chips
- condiments
- cookbooks
- cookie jars
- cookie sheets
- cookies
- crackers
- cutting boards
- flour
- food containers
- food storage bags
- herbs
- lunch/cooler bags
- menus

- muffin tins
- napkins
- pans
- paper plates
- paper towels
- pasta
- pet food
- pet supplies
- phone books
- pitchers
- plastic wrap
- portable cart
- pots
- recycling bins
- rolling pins
- root vegetables
- serving trays
- small appliances
- spices
- trash bags
- vases

long, shallow shelves inside. They are ideal for storing spices and canned goods.

A more traditional pantry cabinet has doors and usually consists of shelves on the inside of the doors, plus either pullout wire shelves or foldout wooden shelves inside. The key is that each shelf is shallow so all items can be seen and food packages don't get lost in the back of the narrow space.

Both types of pantries are usually available as base cabinets or tall cabinets. With the latter, they are typically ordered to match the height of your refrigerator or upper cabinets. Full-height lazy Susan systems are also available for corner pantries.

Closet Fact: The Hoosier cabinet—first developed by the Hoosier Manufacturing Company in Indiana—was a fixture in American kitchens a century ago. Billed as "a pantry and kitchen in one," its sales were geared toward rural families.

Options: If You Don't Have Room for a Full Pantry

1 Fold-out pantries incorporate several layers of shelving, beginning with the backs of the doors. Store frequently used items in the front and items that you use less often toward the rear. Pivot either hinged shelf to get to rear shelving.

2 Pullout pantries can be installed in wall, base, or floor-to-ceiling cabinets. This narrow base-cabinet pullout is ideal for spices, condiments, or vitamins.

3 This reach-in pantry is tucked out of the way in the corner but is conveniently close to the food-prep area. Glass doors and interior lighting let you see what you're after before opening the doors. Among other things, it houses the cookbook collection.

AFTER

This pantry reorganization made items easier to find and to reach. Note that one shelf was removed in order to install the pullout bins, helper shelf, and lazy Susan. Tall, clear containers consolidate cereals, pastas, nuts, and dried fruits.

BEFORE

Pantry Storage Strategies

T ry not to store items where you can't see them, such as behind boxed or bagged goods. Putting larger items toward the back of a shelf and smaller items up front will help. Tiered inserts are a good solution, too. They allow you to view all of the contents on a shelf or in a cabinet. Because the tiers raise each successive row of goods from front to back, there's no need to pull out every soup can to grab the one you want. Another solution is to store dry goods in long, deep, clear containers. The contents will be visible, and you can minimize or eliminate having to put some items where they can't be seen. If clear containers are not available, use labels so you know the contents without having to pull an item off the shelf. Remember, visibility is a great memory prompter. If you can't see it, you may forget you have it.

Smart Tip

Gather the items you only use at certain times of the year, such as the Santa bowls. Put each group in a separate box, and label them. Store the boxes in the pantry, closet, garage, or basement. Designate a shelf in your kitchen for seasonal items, and rotate them out of their boxes and onto the shelf when you need them.

Options: Four Ways to Make Pantry Goods Easier to Grab

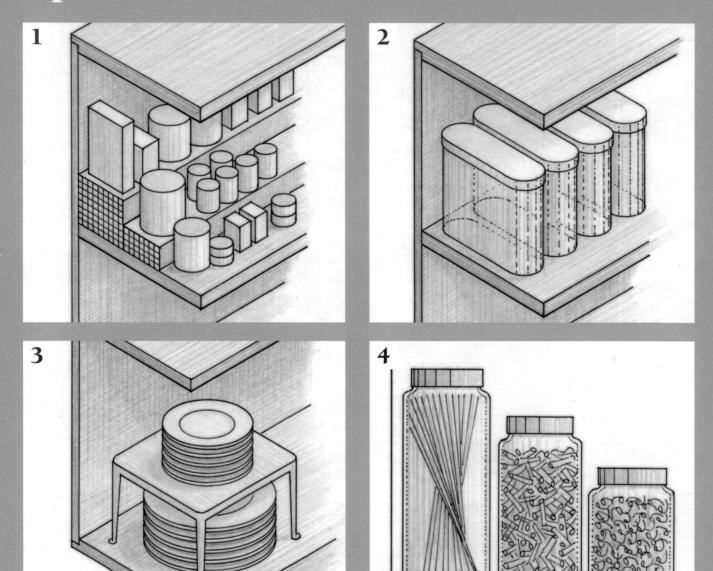

1 Tiers. Tiers allow you to see what's in store behind the first row of your pantry. You can buy tiered shelf inserts at many home-good stores, or you can build them for little or no cost. To see how, turn to page 100.

2 Clear containers. Elongated, clear containers like these make good use of cabinet space and allow you to see what you have. They're ideal for pantry staples, such as cereal and pasta. Always choose food containers that have airtight lids. (See the photo on the opposite page.)

3 Helper shelves. Helper shelves, which can be seen in the lower right of the photo on the opposite page, make it easy to reach the dinner plates in your walk-in pantry without having to remove the dessert plates first. Many models are available, or you can build your own. To see how, turn to page 100.

4 Proper placement. When loading a pantry cabinet, put the tallest items toward the back, as shown in this section view. That way, you can see smaller items up front, but the taller items remain visible.

Clear containers and wire bins keep stored items visible and easy to locate.

How To: Build Tiered and Helper Shelves

Tiered shelves don't increase storage capacity, but they make it easier to see and access the items you have. The shelf heights in the version shown below and opposite top are 1¾ and 4¼ inches tall. When cutting to length, each shelf should be ⅛ inch less than the cabinet width, or you may not be able to maneuver the assembly into position.

Helper shelves increase the capacity *and* accessibility of cabinets by providing two shelves in the place of one. They are typically used on one side of the cabinet only, keeping the other side free for taller items. This project (bottom and opposite bottom) uses a ½ x 8 x 12-inch plywood shelf on two ¾ x 5½ x 8-inch supports, but you can vary dimensions.

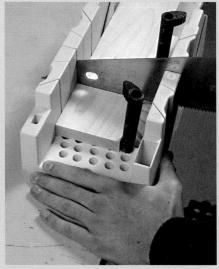

1 Cut 1x4 tier supports 3½ in. and 1 in. high. Cut 1x4 tier shelves to the width of your cabinet. A miter box ensures square crosscuts.

2 A table saw or miter saw (shown) is a faster, easier way to make the saw cuts required for the projects shown on this page.

3 Using a pneumatic nailer or hammer, nail the shelves to the supports. Apply glue to ensure long-lasting joints.

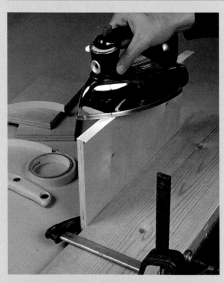

1 Attach edging veneer to the helper shelf by applying heat. A clamp holds the workpiece so you can keep hands clear of the iron.

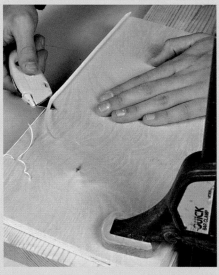

2 Trim excess veneer using a utility knife or block plane, and finish the edge with a sanding block for an invisible joint.

3 With the shelf clamped to the sides, drill pilot holes using a countersink bit, and attach the pieces with 1½-in. flathead screws.

COMPLETED PROJECT

Tiered shelves for soups, sauces, and other small containers may be used on a shelf (left) or countertop. They are available at many home stores. You don't have to purchase one, however. Building one (opposite top) is a simple DIY project.

Helper shelves, increase pantry-cabinet storage capacity by giving you a second shelf above your existing one. They are available in many styles and materials. You can also make your own for almost no cost (right and opposite bottom).

COMPLETED PROJECT

COMPLETED PROJECT

Subdivided drawers allow the spices, utensils, and liquid seasonings in this pullout pantry (top left) to each have their own sections. Dividers, organizers, and spice drawers keep these typical pantry items (left) from mingling. Add your own dividers to any drawer (above and opposite).

Pantry Drawers

In walk-in or reach-in pantries, it's helpful to include drawers for storing table linens, cutlery, spices, and more. Wide, shallow drawers are good for utensils and other kitchen gadgets. Avoid deep drawers for these items because they will just end up piled on top of one another. On the other hand, deep drawers are perfect for pots and pans, dishes, and small appliances. Make extensive use of adjustable drawer dividers or dish caddies to keep items separated. Drawer inserts can help you establish one specific spot for each knife, ladle, or spice jar. Adjustable pegs and pegboard inserts work well for storing dishes. If you have old drawers that don't pull out all the way, look into replacing the drawer boxes with new ones that will accommodate full-extension slides. You should be able to reuse your old drawer fronts.

Saving MONEY

A pantry cabinet that is used for storing large items, especially in significant quantities (including rolls of paper towels, 2-liter bottles of soda, and boxes of cereal), doesn't require expensive pullout hardware. Deep shelves work just fine.

How To: Build Dividers for Drawers

It's not often you can solve two problems with one stroke, but adding dividers to drawers will do just that. First, dividers keep items in their places so that it's easy to find them. Second, the dividers will solve a common problem with many inexpensive drawers—sagging drawer bottoms. The insert acts as a stiffener once it's installed with screws. In addition, waiting to add drawer organizers until after you finish a remodeling gives more time to determine your exact needs so that you can configure them just the way you want. It will also save you some money.

1 Cut stock ½ x 2-in. pine, sold at most home centers, to length using a miter box and handsaw (shown) or a miter saw. You may also use plywood, in which case see page 100 on applying edging veneer.

2 Assemble the pieces with glue and No. 17 1-in. brads. Wipe off excess glue immediately using a damp cloth. Apply a coat of water-based (acrylic) varnish before installation.

3 Place the assembly in the drawer, and mark its location as shown. Remove the insert, and drill three holes for the mounting screws between your marks.

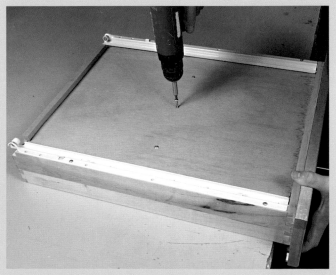

4 Attach the organizer using three 1-in. flathead screws driven through predrilled holes in the drawer bottom. Use a block of scrap wood to hold the insert tight against the bottom while installing the screws.

Think of the Fridge as a Cold Closet

The refrigerator is one "closet" that virtually no one can do without. Keeping it organized is imperative to an efficient kitchen.

When buying a new refrigerator, look for shelves that allow you to adjust their heights according to your needs. Height-adjustable door bins are also useful. A few newer fridges have motorized shelves that go up and down with the push of a button. Others have half-width shelves, so you can adjust one side for taller items. Pullout bins are a good feature; use one to keep condiments and sauces together and accessible.

If your refrigerator doesn't have all the bells and whistles you'd like, invest in some inexpensive space-saving devices. A two-tier can dispenser holds a dozen 12-ounce cans, which roll forward for easy access. Don't want that gallon of milk to take up so much

Half-width shelves allow you to adjust accordingly. Keep shelves apart for tall soda bottles. Keep them closer together when storing small condiment jars. Accessories, including soda-can dispensers and a wine rack that clamps under a shelf, may also be used to maximize the space in your "cold" closet.

room? A thin gallon jug—it's less than 3 inches wide—nestles in along the sidewall. A wine rack hangs from the bottom of a wire shelf. And, of course, there are the old storage standbys, including lazy Susans for small condiment bottles and clear, stackable containers for deli meats and cheeses.

For freezers, which often come without any shelving, buy an after-market wire or stainless-steel shelf. Newer models have tilt-out door bins that allow you to store bags of frozen vegetables and other small items without fear of an avalanche. With the right mix of features, your freezer storage will be much more efficient.

Where the Wine Lives

Certain types of wine benefit from age. If you've got a number of those in your collection, you'll require a long-term storage solution. If you're an avid collector, it's probably best to have a wine cellar where you can keep several hundred on hand. If your collection isn't so grand, consider a refrigerated wine cellar. You can get everything from a unit designed to fit under a kitchen counter that holds as few as 18 bottles to a floor-to-ceiling model that stores 150.

A wine refrigerator keeps temperatures low enough and maintains the high humidity level that is ideal for fine wines. Full-extension shelves make bottles easy to access.

The "pantry drawer" of this new bottom-mount refrigerator makes it easy for kids to reach fruit, yogurt, and other healthy snacks—and the dividers keep items organized. With the dividers removed, the drawer can accommodate large party platters and deli trays. Both full-width bottom compartments (the other is a freezer) fully extend.

Closet organizing components allow you to create wine and beverage centers, such as this basement wine cellar and entertainment center.

Closets on a Budget

Chapter 8

THERE ARE LOTS OF WAYS to add or reorganize closets inexpensively. They will involve some manual labor, perhaps learning a few new skills, and using your creativity. You may also need to forgo fixed notions about what constitutes a closet. One strategy is to add freestanding closets. You can buy one ready to assemble, or build one using our plan. The third approach is a closet without walls. We'll look at all the possibilities.

Freestanding closets can be traditional (opposite and above) or more contemporary (left) in style. Both types are less expensive and less permanent than framing a new closet from scratch. However they are also limited in the amount of items they can store.

The Freestanding Solution

There are two types of freestanding closets: European-style wardrobes and traditional furniture-type closets. Both are usually less expensive than building a new closet with lumber, enclosing it with drywall and a door, and then adding organizers. Moreover, both can be taken with you when you move.

EUROPEAN-STYLE WARDROBES

European-style wardrobes resemble tall boxes with sliding doors. Some are quite pricey and are made with beautiful materials and finishes. Knockoffs, such as those available from IKEA, are less costly and are designed to accom-

modate various organizing components, such as shelves, drawers, pullouts, and racks.

FURNITURE-TYPE CLOSETS

Furniture closets take more traditional forms and are often raised off the floor by short legs. Wardrobes, armoires, cabinets, clothes presses, clothes cupboards, chests, lockers, and trunks may all serve as closets. Some combine clothing rods and drawers on the inside; others are simply outfitted with pegs, hooks, or shelves. The common trait is all can be closed with a door. Such closets can be purchased new or may be found at flea markets and garage sales.

Smart Tip

A quick, easy, and inexpensive way to add drawers to a reach-in or walk-in closet is to find a secondhand dresser (or an inexpensive new one) that you can fit into your closet design.

This freestanding wardrobe includes a rod and four adjustable shelves. One door is mirrored, which comes in handy when trying on clothes.

Closet Material Costs

ITEM	DIMENSION	PRICE PER FOOT
Pine shelving	¾ x 12 in.	$1.90
Wire shelf	20 in. deep	$2.50
Wire shelf w/rod	12 in. deep	$4.25
MDF melamine*	⅝-in. sheet	$1.20**
PB melamine	¾ x 11¼-in. shelves	$1.70
Steel rod	1-in. dia., adjustable	$1.25
Round stock	1½-in. dia.	$2.60

Price varies depending upon grade, gauge, and length

* Laminate on two sides   ** Per sq. ft.

PB = particleboard

Closet Fact: Built-in wall closets were uncommon prior to World War II, when chests, trunks, and wall-mounted pegs typically provided storage. After the war, however, closets were incorporated into new house designs. It's been suggested that closet space was a key factor in the migration of people to the suburbs.

Built-in wardrobes install like kitchen cabinets and are affixed to the wall. You can fit them out with components that you build yourself. See the following pages for step-by-step instructions and diagrams.

Build a Box

If you can build a box, you can build a freestanding closet. Use ¾-inch lumber-core plywood for the sides, top, bottom, and doors; and use ¼-inch plywood for the back. Building a closet gives you the option of custom arranging shelves and cubbies. You can also hang a mirror on the back of the door. Finish the closet to complement the rest of the room.

Building Your Own Wardrobe

If you plan to build a freestanding or built-in wardrobescratch, you will find several options in the "panel goods" aisle at your local home center. The least expensive is particleboard finished with paper or melamine laminates. Slightly more expensive, but less apt to chip or dent, is medium density fiberboard (MDF). It can be ordered with a melamine laminate, or you can paint it. Grade A and B veneer plywood, if purchased by the sheet, costs more than MDF and will need to be stained or painted. Finishing is labor intensive and adds to the cost because you'll need sandpaper and painting supplies, but plywood does not require the special joint fasteners that fiberboard does, and it will stand up to heavy usage and to being moved.

Tools you will need. In addition to a basic collection of hand tools, you'll need a good circular saw, clamps, saw horses, an orbital sander, a drill, and a good assortment of bits. If the plan from which you build involves rabbeted joints or dadoes for shelving, you'll also need a router or a table saw and chisels. These tools will pay for themselves many times over during the course of a lifetime, but if you're not ready to make the investment, it may make sense to buy a ready-to-assemble closet. For that, all you need is a screwdriver and a hammer. The manufacturer typically supplies the requisite Allen wrench.

How To: Build Your Own Wardrobe Components

If you have the time and skills, you can build many closet organization components yourself. In the sequence below we show you how to add a hanger bar to the inside of plywood or fiberboard door. Use the bar for hanging garments while assembling an outfit or for storing belts, ties, and the like. You'll note that the bars are fastened to the door in such a way as to avoid seeing the screwhead on the finished door. Employ similar techniques to build door pulls. Simply glue the pulls to the stand-off dowels, and drive the screws through the back of the door as shown in the illustration at right.

Building the Hanger Bars

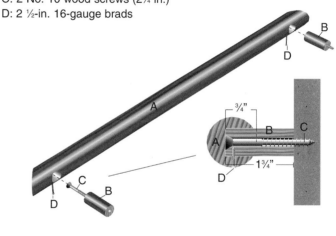

Hanger-Bar Materials **(for back of door on page 109)**

A: 1 pc. 1⅛-in.-dia. x length to suit dowel
B: 2 pcs. ¾-in.-dia. x 1¾-in. dowel
C: 2 No. 10 wood screws (2¼ in.)
D: 2 ½-in. 16-gauge brads

1 To ensure hole alignment when building the handles or hanger bar, draw a line the full length of the dowel using a simple jig.

2 Bore holes square to the dowel using a drill press. Inexpensive drill stands that allow you to mount your drill are available.

3 Test the standoffs for fit. Then rest them on blocks of wood so that the dowel is parallel with the miter box. Saw the ends to 45 deg.

The plans for the pullout pants hanger, below, are surprisingly simple. There is no fancy hardware required. The same idea can be used to build pullout shelves. Just substitute plywood for the dowels. Assemble the shelf components before installation. The 3-inch spacing between dowels allows ample spacing for hanging clothing.

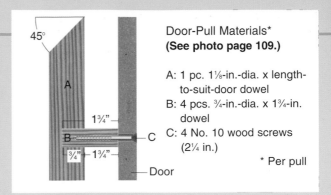

45°

Door-Pull Materials*
(See photo page 109.)

A: 1 pc. 1⅛-in.-dia. x length-to-suit-door dowel
B: 4 pcs. ¾-in.-dia. x 1¾-in. dowel
C: 4 No. 10 wood screws (2¼ in.)

* Per pull

1¾"
¾" 1¾"
Door

Building the Pants Pullout Rack

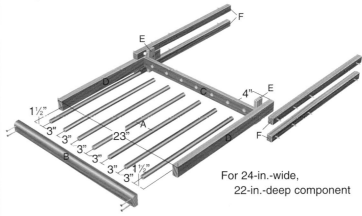

Pants-Pullout Materials*

A: 7 pcs. ½-in.-dia. x 16¾-in dowel
B: 1 pc. ¾ x 2 x 23 in.
C: 1 pc. ¾ x 2 x 21½ in.
D: 2 pcs. ¾ x 2 x 20¾ in.
E: 2 pcs. ⅜ x 1½ x 3¼-in. plywood
F: 4 pcs. ¾ x ¾ x 21½ in.
8 No. 10 wood screws (2¼ in.)
16 No. 10 wood screws (1½ in.)*

1½" 3" 3" 3" 23" 3" 3" 1½" 4"
For 24-in.-wide, 22-in.-deep component

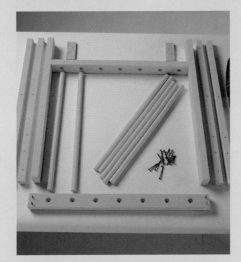

1 Here are the pieces you'll need to build your own pants pullout component. Assemble with glue and screws as shown in the diagram.

2 The pullout slides between two cleats. Before screwing in the top one, insert two pieces of cardboard to create a small gap.

3 Bore a hole at the front end of the top cleat, and insert a shelf peg or short piece of dowel. It will act as a stop In concert with part E.

Smart Tip

When there's no room for a closet at the front or back door, keep one (or two) coat racks close by for hanging coats, scarves, leashes, and hats. The racks typically come with 4 to 6 S-shaped hooks, each of which can accommodate a coat or jacket. Look for a model that will be stable under full loads. A metal ring near the bottom of the rack will corral umbrellas and ensure long-lasting and sturdy performance. Coat racks may also be used in a bedroom to hang clothes you intend to wear again before laundering.

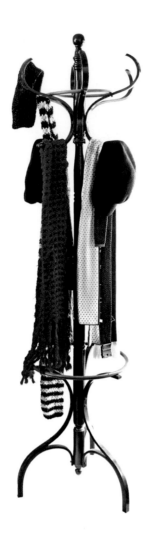

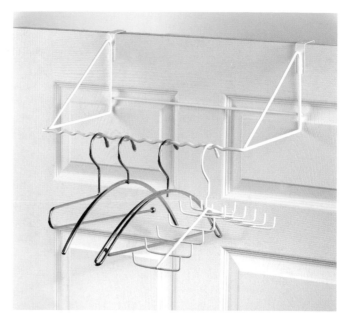

This simple wire rack hangs over a door, creating useful storage space in an otherwise underutilized area. It's a great place to air out clothes before putting them back in the closet.

Closet Fact: Before closets, hollowed logs fitted with lids served as clothing storage. With the advent of improved woodworking tools, six-sided rudimentary trunks—today's equivalent of a blanket box—gained popularity.

Creating "Closets" Out of Thin Air

Whether it's a bedroom, kitchen, or hallway, there's often a need—but no space—for a closet. In such cases, you can often find space on walls and near floor and ceiling areas to store items.

In the bedroom, it may be a clothing rod mounted from a wall or ceiling and screened off from the room with a shoji divider. A simple garment bag hung from an attic rafter can store off-season garments. In the kitchen, a pot rack hung above the sink or over a kitchen island can store pots, pans, and utensils that would otherwise fill a pantry shelf or base cabinet. In the hallway, it may be a clothes tree or a long peg rack that buys you extra storage space.

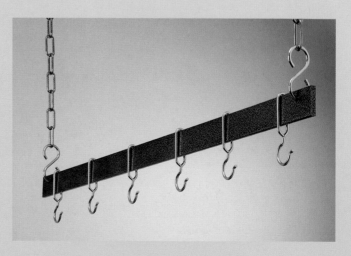

This tall upholstered headboard is backed by a mirror and closet rod. It supplements storage in a nearby wardrobe.

Saving MONEY

A cheap and simple closet can consist of a freestanding rack hidden from view by a folding screen or curtain. It is available in both utilitarian and ornate styles, with or without casters. Casters let you push the rack into the corner when not in use.

Is space tight? A simple bar with S-hooks attached to two chains (opposite) works fine as a pot hanger, or you can use a steel bar mounted behind a window valance (near right). A cart on casters (far right) can be wheeled into the kitchen when you've got work to do and can be used to store frequently used items.

Options: Three Low-Cost Closet Accessories

1 **Shoe pockets.** This canvas organizer can store 10 pairs of shoes on the back of a narrow, 24-inch door. If you prefer to see more of your shoes to make selection easier, over-the-door wire racks are also available.

2 **Standard-hung baskets.** Ideal for the back of pantry or utility closet doors, the standards are screwed directly to the door. A variety of organizers can be mounted in the slots, including baskets, paper-towel holders, purse hooks, and shoe and slipper racks.

3 **Hanging shelves.** These "soft" shelves can store folded garments or boots. They're especially good for stacking sweaters. Only buy the products that are stiffened with a wire frame at the top. Organizers that are stiffened with cardboard will sag. Hanging shelves are available in smaller "cubby" sizes, too. They're perfect for storing shoes, sandals, and other small items. If the extra load of hung shelves causes your rod to deflect—a real possibility—add extra support. A notched wooden pole fit under the rod works well.

How To: Bring Order to Sandals, Slippers, and Flip-flops

1 Insert the hooks through the slots on the bamboo rack, and then mount the rack over the door.

2 Stretch the elastic strap and hook to the door bottom. This model will fit various door heights.

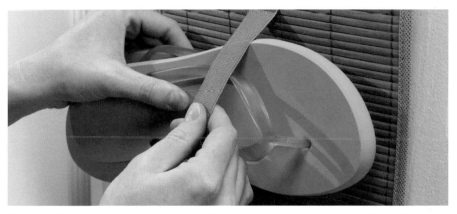

3 Use the elastic strap that runs down the rack to secure sandals, slippers, caps, scarves, and more. The rack can hold up to 10 pairs of flip-flops.

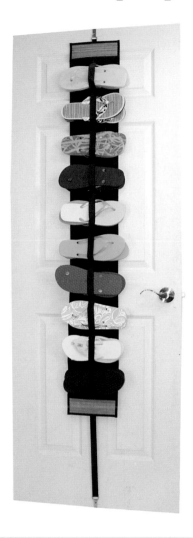

Over the Door

Components that make use of unutilized space, and that are not too costly, are a great way to increase closet efficiency on a budget. One of the most popular ways to do this is with an over-the-door organizer. Once limited to plastic shoe bags, dozens of offerings are now available. Some are for storing specific items, such as baseball caps, sandals, gift-wrapping supplies, and video games. Others are for general storage, such as standard-mounted baskets, shelves, and racks. Tip: the door upon which the organizer is hung can be any door. The back of a bedroom door is a popular location. Door-mounted organizers are also commonly found on laundry, utility, and pantry doors.

Saving MONEY

Hanging soft shelves and canvas shoe organizers on an existing closet rod will save money compared with installing new fiberboard or wire organizers. It will also add a lot of weight. A quick, cheap solution is to prop the rod with a notched wooden pole, as shown.

Utility, Garage, and Basement Closets

Chapter 9 **HARDWORKING CLOSETS** are in a class by themselves. They may be called upon to store harsh chemicals, hold heavy loads, and survive accidental impact, moisture, cold, and heat. They must also organize a wildly diverse assortment of items, from cleansers to hedge trimmers. Such closets include storage areas in the kitchen, garage, and basement. They even find their way outdoors in the form of closet-size sheds.

Use the garage wall to reclaim space for your cars (top). Some systems (opposite and above) can be used to store large or small items.

Utility closets must be versatile enough to store a wide range of items. This simple arrangement handles bulk supplies, pet food, a vacuum, an ironing board, and more.

Utility Closets: Function Over Fancy

The utility closet is where you turn when the power is out, the pet needs feeding, a child drops a glass of milk, or you need a new liner for the trash can. It is relied upon to store cleaning equipment, cleaning supplies, and other items that are necessary to run a modern household.

A house can have more than one utility closet. You may have one near the kitchen and another near the laundry. Nor does it need to be a full-fledged closet. A large cabinet and a couple of deep drawers may be all you need.

A utility closet that's close to the kitchen may be used to store cleaning products, paper towels, rags, brooms, dustpans, sponges, and the like. If it's big enough, it may also hold a fold-up step stool, a basic tool kit, recyclables, and pet food. In the garage, a utility closet may contain flashlights and candles for when the power goes out, tools and miscellaneous hardware, car vacuums, tire pumps, and implements for car washing and waxing.

Closet Fact: Clara Barton, founder of the American Red Cross, had 38 closets in her house—all filled with donated supplies in preparation for future calamities.

Chemicals

Cleansers, plant fertilizers, pesticides, and the like are often toxic and are best stored outside the living area of your home, in the garage or basement. A lockable freestanding closet is a good solution. Store only the cleaning products you use frequently in the kitchen or bathroom, and equip doors with childproof latches. Organize everyday cleaning supplies in a plastic caddy or a pullout bin.

BEFORE

Junk drawers are often where you try to put whatever doesn't fit in the utility closet. Nearly every kitchen has one. Add drawer dividers to keep yours organized.

AFTER

BROOM CLOSETS

Broom closets for brooms and vacuums are typically custom built to fill gaps between cabinet runs and the wall or between large appliances and the wall. While this is an appropriate way to use leftover space, broom closets are often too small for everything we try to pack into them.

To make cleaning chores a little more pleasant, keep your closet well organized. Weed out items that are better stored elsewhere, and then get as many things as possible off the closet floor. Use hooks or a wall rack to hang your brooms, mops, and dusters, as well as smaller items, such as dustpans and fly swatters. Use the space you've opened up on the floor to store a small vacuum cleaner, mop bucket, or tool kit. A hook, such as one made for hanging bicycles, installed above your vacuum cleaner can help keep the hose and electrical cord from becoming entangled.

Don't have a broom closet? Try hanging mops and brooms on the wall behind a door, the wall of a basement stairway, or in the space between the refrigerator and the wall. (Slide-out broom racks that work great for narrow spaces are available.) If you have a walk-in pantry or laundry room, devote a section to cleaning supplies.

BULK SUPPLIES

As mentioned earlier, buying supplies in bulk is a good way to save money. Just don't use prime closet space to store them. Closets for bulk supplies are best located in a basement or garage. They can be shallow; 12 inches deep will hold a large package of paper towels or toilet paper and accommodate three rows of canned goods.

Don't Forget...

When designing a utility closet, make a list of what it must store. Here are some suggestions to get you started.

- batteries
- brooms
- brushes
- buckets
- caddies
- candles
- car-cleaning sup-
  plies
- cleaning products
- cleaning towels
- dustpans
- extension cords
- feather dusters
- first-aid kits
- flashlights
- fly swatters
- goggles
- ladders
- lightbulbs
- mops
- paper towels

- pet food
- pet supplies
- polishes
- rags
- recycling bins
- rubber gloves
- scrubbers
- sponges
- step stools
- tool boxes with
  frequently used
  tools
- trash bags
- vacuum accesso-
  ries
- vacuum cleaners
- waxes

Keep the broom and dust-pan (left) and vacuum (above) from underfoot by storing them in narrow closets, such as these. Both closets shown here were built into leftover spaces that are less than a foot wide (left) or deep (above).

Smart Tip

Keep frequently used tools in a broom closet or other utility closet. A screwdriver with multiple bits stored in the handle will cover most household needs, along with a small hammer, measuring tape, needle-nose pliers, adjustable wrench, utility knife, staple gun, duct tape, glue, pencil, and a flashlight. Store them in a small toolbox or caddy.

How To: Install a Track-and-Hook System

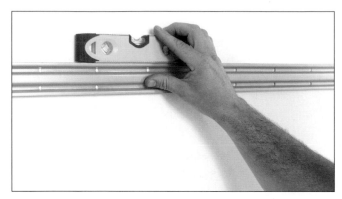

1 Draw a level line on the wall at the desired height. Find a stud in the wall near one end. Align the track with the line, and screw it to the stud. Check for level.

2 Install remaining fasteners. The predrilled holes will align with stud locations. A cordless drill-driver speeds up the job.

3 Snap the plastic cover over the steel track. It's not only decorative—it also prevents users from cutting their fingers on the track's edges.

4 Snap hooks and other organizing components on the track as needed. No fasteners are required, so parts are easily rearranged to maximize the available space.

Garages and Basements

Storage in these spaces serves two functions. One is to organize items that you use in the garage or basement, such as workshop tools. The other is to store things that would otherwise jam up your house closets, such as camping equipment. In the first case, items need to be accessible. A bicycle tire pump, for example, should be easy to grab at a moment's notice. In the second case, the storage can be out of the way on high shelving, accessible only by a step stool. Think of this storage as a sort of closet for your house, a place to put off-season and little-used items.

Closet organizing systems designed for garages and basements are often subject to more abuse and dirt than those designed for interior closets. Consequently, look for systems with epoxy powder coatings rather than melamine or paper laminates. Epoxy powder coatings are baked on. The coating is less apt to peel, chip, or crack (each of which can lead to corrosion in a steel system). It's also easier to clean. Epoxy coatings are available on both wire and fiberboard components. In high-moisture areas, however, wire shelving promotes better ventilation and is less likely to suffer when it gets wet than are fiberboard products.

Track-and-hook systems (opposite) are strong enough to support wall and base cabinets. Include a work surface for making repairs and building small projects.

AFTER

This garage reorganization took only a few hours. The sturdy track system sports clever holders that can be used for everything from gardening tools to a wet-dry vacuum. You may also hang shelves from it. This system works well for unfinished basements, too, because it requires fewer holes to be drilled than rail-and- standard systems—a real time-saver when putting fasteners in masonry.

BEFORE

Smart Tip

The garage and basement are good places to keep a donation bin. Lauren Spahr, an organizing expert at Rubbermaid, says that having a bin available at all times makes it easier to take action when you find something you would like to donate. Plus, it benefits people and the environment.

Modular garage cabinets can be arranged in a variety of ways (above and opposite bottom). If you're using the space as a workshop, limit open shelving to keep sawdust off your tools and supplies. This system is epoxy coated—inside, outside, and on all edges—to better resist moisture.

Saving MONEY

Stackable plastic bins are a quick and inexpensive way to create neat, dust-free storage in a garage, attic, or basement. Use them for fertilizers and potting soil, holiday ornaments and light strings, cooking equipment that's rarely used, and the like. They keep moisture and dirt out, too. Just remember to apply contents labels so you know what's inside each bin.

If you have a deck that's raised at least 5 ft., the space beneath it may be suitable for storage. This below-deck area houses power equipment and a workspace.

A full-size shed can store outdoor power equipment and gardening tools, along with fuels, pesticides, and solvents that should not be stored in or near the house.

Outdoor "Closets"

A shed, when you think about it, is nothing more than an outdoor closet. What's more, it can be organized with the same closet organizing systems you'd use in a garage or basement. Like indoor closets, outdoor closets can be walk-in or reach-in. If space is limited, a reach-in shed built against the house or garage—also called a backpack, lean-to, or vertical shed—is the best solution. The footprint can be as little as 2 x 6 feet and still help you organize dozens of tools and supplies. If you have the space, sheds can be whatever size you wish, but if you keep it under 10 x 10 feet, you won't have to worry about zoning setbacks or getting a building permit.

In place of closet rods, outdoor closets should have hanger rails for storing long-handled tools, such as spades and rakes. Shelves are better than drawers because enclosed outdoors spaces are favored by insects and rodents. Use solid wood shelving, not fiberboard products. Or use epoxy powder-coated wire systems for their durability and ease of cleaning.

Plastic bins with lids are a great way to store many of the items that end up in a shed, including fertilizers, seat cushions, toys, and life jackets. Use track-and-hook storage systems, such as the one on page 120, to store gardening tools, sprayers, sprinklers, and the like.

This outdoor kitchen shed houses a grill, refrigerator, microwave, cooking utensils, and dinnerware. When not in use, bifold doors keep out the elements.

This double-wall, vinyl lean-to shed (far left) has pre-formed holes into which hangers for pegboard (left) or other organizers may be hung.

Closets That Do More

Chapter 10

SOME CLOSETS ARE CALLED UPON to serve special needs. They store hobby paraphernalia, craft materials, office supplies, toys and games, and holiday decorations. Still other closets are asked to do more than store things. They serve as virtual rooms for laundries, home offices, entertainment equipment, wet bars, and bedrooms. (Well, at least the bed.)

Specialty closets, such as this one for toys in a family room, must be versatile enough to store a wide variety of items.

Smart Tip

Children generally don't need a lot of space to do their thing. If you live in tight quarters and can spare a closet, convert it into a mini play space, reading nook, or art center. Put shelving up high; install plenty of lighting; and use the walls for chalkboards, magnet boards, and hanging artwork. Attach a plywood board to the wall with a cleat and a piano hinge so that it can fold down and serve as a worktable. Use a fold-out bracket to support the table. Install carpet padding and carpet on the floor, and supply cushions to make it comfy.

Specialty Closets

Specialty closets are defined by very specific needs. If you sew, make jewelry, enjoy oil painting, or simply work on a computer, it's nice to have a place where you can access equipment and supplies quickly and easily. If you're a model railroader, you'll need a spot to make repairs and construct layout accessories. Collect stamps or coins? A closet study is ideal because you can close (and lock) the door when you're finished. Need storage for toys and games? A specialty closet may be your answer.

Specialty closets, such as this office, are often of the open variety, where closet organizing components are used in the room at large, not hidden by an enclosure or door.

Smart Tip

Wall organizing systems, typically found in a garage or basement workshop, work great in a craft room. This one is versatile and easy to install, and it helps keep things organized.

Thinking outside the box, a homeowner used these closet-organizing components to create a craft center for the entire family. The pullout table (left and opposite) is great for wrapping gifts or drawing projects.

ORGANIZING A CRAFT CENTER

In a craft center, the same organizing principles used in kitchen design apply. Put things close to where you'll use them. The scissors, tape, wrapping paper, and ribbons go near where you wrap gifts. Your collection of oil colors, easels, and brushes goes near where you paint canvases. Reserve counters and the walls just above them for items you use frequently. It's your most valuable storage space, so don't waste it. Put dividers in drawers so that contents don't become jumbled and difficult to find. There's nothing worse than losing a creative moment during a search for the right palette knife. Install pullout shelves where possible. They save you from having to pull everything off a shelf to retrieve an item buried in the back.

A scrapbook station doesn't require a lot of space. The same plan can be used for bead work, coin and stamp collecting, and many other hobbies.

An "open closet" craft center, such as this sewing area, requires an assortment of shelves, cubbies, and drawers, along with a solid work surface.

Closet organizers are ideal for making your laundry area more convenient. Choose fine mesh shelves, and include a hanger rod. Reserve floor space for laundry baskets.

LAUNDRIES

Doing the laundry is no fun, but with the right organization it can at least be as efficient as possible. A sorting table is essential. If space is limited, buy a small folding table. A clothes rod is very handy. It allows you to pull shirts and pants from the dryer while they are still slightly damp and hang them to complete the drying process. Doing so saves ironing. If you have the space, install extra rods or a clothesline for drying, and skip the gas or electric dryer all together. Install wire shelves directly over the washing machine when possible for storing detergents and bleaches. Don't forget to leave space for a trash can that can be lined with a plastic garbage bag. You will need an easy way to dispose of lint that builds up on your lint filter and to empty bits of trash from pockets.

Security Closets

Closets used to store valuables, such as coin collections and jewelry, or potentially dangerous items, such as weapons and toxic chemicals, need to be secure. You can do this by installing a security door and reinforcing the doorjamb and closet itself.

Security doors often have a fiberglass or wood finish and therefore don't look much different from other doors, but they are solid core and clad with steel. If the gap between the door and the frame is more than $\frac{1}{16}$ inch, reinforce the jamb and stops. First, carefully remove the door-stop trim. Then drive several screws through the doorjamb into the nearest studs, particularly around the hinge and lock locations. This reinforcement makes it harder to pry the frame and release a latch or bolt from its keeper. Use screws at least 3 inches long so that they reach well into the studs. Avoid driving them too deeply, or the jamb may bow. You can now reinstall the door-stop trim over the screws. Next, line the interior of the closet with $\frac{1}{2}$-inch plywood. Use screws to fasten the plywood over the existing drywall and into the wall studs.

If the hinges of the door you want to secure are to the outside (that is, the door swings into the living space), an intruder only needs to pull the hinge pins to gain entry. Either change the hinges and door to inswinging, or install security hinges with nonremovable hinge pins or hinge studs designed to prevent door removal.

Install a strong dead-bolt lock, too. The bolt and the key cylinder should be solid. The stronger the lock, the longer it will take to break—and most intruders won't spend more than a minute attempting to gain entry.

Divide and conquer kids' toys by keeping out only what they actually use. Store board games in original boxes on shelves (top), and put large, bulky items, such as stuffed animals and sporting equipment, in wire bins (above).

TOYS AND GAMES

Toys can overrun a home. It seems there are never enough shelves or drawers to contain them. Stackable bins are one good solution. Buy clear ones or label the outside so you know which has the blocks and which has the art supplies. Then stick to this rule with children: you can't pull out another bin until you've picked up and put away the contents of the one with which you're playing.

Game storage. Games are a bit easier to store. If you keep the original box in good shape (reinforce box top corners with clear packing tape), games can be stacked on shelves. If the boxes are gone, put the pieces in resealable plastic bags, and clip them to the game boards. Install vertical dividers on your shelving, and devote one slot to each game. Donate games your children have outgrown!

HOLIDAY DECORATIONS

Use large wire shelves or racks in a basement, attic, or garage to keep your collections of lights and ornaments organized and in good condition. Wrap fragile items, such as ornaments, in tissue paper, and store them in boxes. Stow holiday lights, wound neatly, in plastic grocery bags, and hang them on wall hooks. Use helper shelves and clamp-on bins to maximize storage.

> **Closet Fact:** The average U.S. consumer spends more than $60 a year on decorations, gift wrap, and cards. What isn't used often winds up in closets.

Deep pullout bins are great for storing bulky supplies. Smaller items can be stored in clear plastic bins and stored on open shelves. Labeled file boxes for family records fit on shelves that are height-adjusted to suit box sizes. Keep a step stool on hand for reaching items stored on high shelves.

HOME-OFFICE SUPPLIES

Office supplies, especially if you work at home and buy in bulk, can easily fill a small closet. Try to find one central location so that you don't have to search several places in the home for the packing-tape dispenser or box of large envelopes when you need one. An ideal arrangement is a reach-in closet fitted with large pullout bins and drawers. The pullouts can hold various sizes of envelopes, packages of printing paper, extra rolls of various tapes and twines, printer cartridges, and bulk packs of pencils and pens.

Small stuff. A couple of drawers, fitted with dividers, can be used to store smaller items, such as paper clips, rubber bands, staples, labels, batteries, and the like. In the recesses at the side of the closet, install a bin—a waste basket will do—to corral tall, narrow items, such as rolls of kraft paper, mailing tubes, T-squares, and yardsticks. Use desk storage only for the supplies you'll need for the next week or two.

Smart Tip

For valuable items, install a fire-resistant, waterproof safe in your closet. Build it into a wall between studs or in the floor between joists so that a thief can't run off with it. Conceal the safe with a mirror, picture, or piece of furniture. Lock options for either type include key locks, electronic locks, combination locks, and even fingerprint readers.

LOWERED

Murphy beds allow you to lift and stow your bed in a closet-like recess, freeing the room for other uses. With the bed raised (opposite), decorative panels hide the mattress and hardware from view.

Rooms in a Closet

The essential elements of a room can sometimes be fit within the confines of a closet. It is, of course, less convenient than a full-size room, but it allows you to live with fewer square feet. Laundries and home offices are the most common uses for a spare closet. Nurseries, media centers, craft and hobby centers, wet bars, libraries, and play spaces are some of the other possibilities.

If you're planning to make a closet do the work of a room, plan on installing plenty of good lighting. Working or playing in a dark closet can be depressing. Recessed lights in the ceiling are ideal because they won't interfere with shelving. (See restrictions about light placement on page 21.) It's OK to use side recesses for shallow shelves, but maintain as much open working surface as possible. Deeper shelves for infrequently used items may be installed behind the knee well of a desk, but allow space to stretch your legs. Be sure to fully utilize the storage capacity of the closet walls for corkboards, wall organizers, hooks, fabric wall pockets, and small wall-mounted containers.

A walk-in laundry closet (opposite, far right) allows the user to take clothes out of the machines, pivot, and tend to the sorting and folding. An overhead bar can be used for hanging clothes to dry. A reach-in laundry closet (opposite) with curtains offers linen storage and a folding table.

A reach-in closet (left), with the doors removed, now hosts a large vanity, a television, and related equipment. The home-office closet (below) is just the right size for paying bills. While you're working at the desk, the file stand can be rolled into the hall for more room.

RAISED

Saving MONEY

Living in less space through smart design and clever organization can minimize mortgage payments and building costs. Consider that the average new home is 2,438 square feet. The average cost is $270,900. That comes to $111 per square foot. Live (and store) in smaller spaces and see big savings.

Closets Where There Were None

Chapter 11

ADDING A NEW CLOSET is not difficult, but It will probably be more costly than reorganizing an existing one. So exhaust all other storage options before taking the plunge. If a new closet is needed, first decide whether you want it to be permanent or temporary. Then decide on the size, which will depend on your needs and the available space. Finally, choose the type of closet that will best suit your needs and budget.

Freestanding closet systems, such as this pole-mounted unit from Ikea, are a fast way to add a new closet. For a more permanent solution that fits seamlessly with your decor, there is the stud-and-drywall approach. This chapter covers the steps involved in building a conventional closet.

Adding a New Closet

There are several ways to add a new closet to your home: purchase a freestanding wardrobe, build in a wardrobe, opt for an "open" closet, build a new closet using conventional methods, or create one out of "found," or leftover, space. The path you take depends on the amount of space you can devote to a closet, your budget, and whether you need a permanent or temporary solution.

A freestanding wardrobe, as mentioned in Chapter 8, is a quick and easy way to add a new closet. Like cabinets, freestanding wardrobes come with the sawing and finishing already done. Small units are only a few feet wide. Multiple units may be used side by side to achieve a closet of any width. Heights range from 60 to 80 inches.

Freestanding wardrobes offer many design opportunities. They can be positioned against a wall to serve as a reach-in closet, as seen in earlier chapters. Or they can be located several feet from a wall, divider fashion, to create, in effect, a walk-in closet. Some freestanding units have no sides or backs. They are supported on floor-to-ceiling poles or on stands made from slotted standards.

Built-in wardrobes are a more permanant solution. They may be carcass-built (like one or more huge cabinets), frame-built, or built behind a wall of sliding doors. Built-in wardrobes tend to make better use of available space than

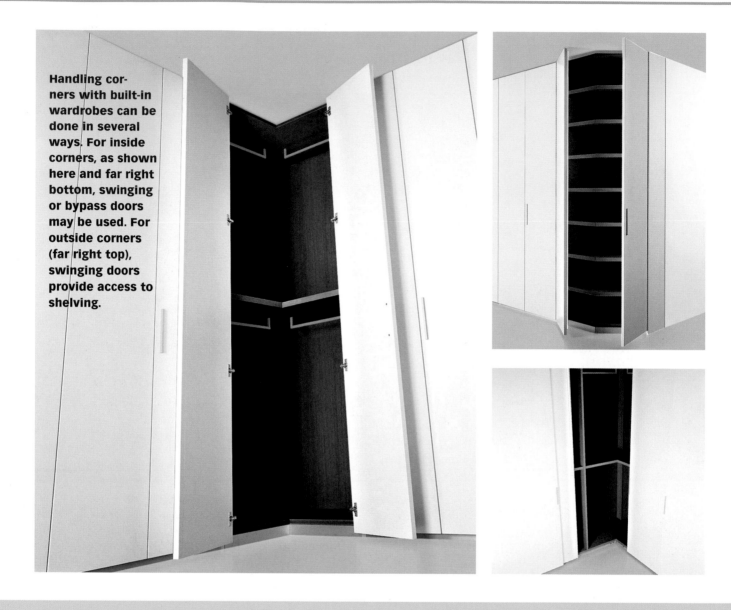

Handling corners with built-in wardrobes can be done in several ways. For inside corners, as shown here and far right bottom, swinging or bypass doors may be used. For outside corners (far right top), swinging doors provide access to shelving.

freestanding wardrobes and are more expensive as well.

Multiple built-ins can be arranged in rows or at angles. If used at right angles, plan ahead for using corner spaces efficiently. Some possibilities for this are shown above.

Open closets are built using closet organizer components but are not enclosed by walls or doors. Think of them as storage places that have escaped the closet and are open to the room. All you need is a corner or an alcove. Common uses include craft centers, media centers, home offices, and bathroom storage.

"Found" spaces can also be converted into closets. This approach can be less expensive than the others be-

An open closet can be situated in an alcove. It has no doors. Here, it is built in an attic, between the roof line and chimney masonry.

A built-in wardrobe can serve as a partition as well as a closet, as shown here. Positioned at one end of the room, units create an area that can be fitted out as a walk-in closet.

cause the enclosure already exists. Common spots include under staircases, at the end of a kitchen cabinet run, or in a wall that fronts a void—typically an attic or the eaves.

Found-space closets need not be small. If you find yourself with a spare room, you can convert it into a walk-in closet, and then turn it back into a bedroom should you want to sell the house. (Bedrooms typically add more to resale than closets.) See the example in the photo at right.

Conventionally framed closets are permanent and are designed to look like part of the house. Stud walls are erected from floor to ceiling, covered with drywall, and painted, and the opening is fitted with the doors of your choice. Trim and door hardware are selected to match the surrounding room. If you want this type of closet, you will have to build one using conventional methods as shown beginning on page 142.

This spare bedroom was converted into a walk-in closet. The bedroom's old reach-in closet is now devoted to shoes.

Open and shut, this magnificent organizer (below and right) serves as both a room divider and a closet in which stored items can be hidden from view. Hardware that slides on tracks as well as pivots makes it possible.

An open closet at one end of a master bathroom (left and opposite) combines with a built-in wardrobe to provide the best of all worlds. Items for which you need immediate access, such as frequently used bath products, towels, and robes, are stored in the open area. Closed storage is better suited to clothing, accessories, and other supplies. Adequate ventilation is a must for closets in moisture-prone areas.

Turn an attic into one giant closet. In addition to clothes, it stores toys, games, and electronics, and serves as a crafts room. The organizers have a tougher laminate surface than what you'd find in a bedroom closet.

Closet Fact: *Closet,* from the Latin term *clausum* ("closed"), originally meant a small private room, often behind a bedroom, where a person could go to read, study, pray, or enjoy works of art. It was for privacy, not storage.

Smart Tip

The easy way to frame a wall is to preassemble it on the floor, and raise it into place. This way you can drive the nails through the plate faces into the studs. When working in existing spaces where floors and ceilings are not parallel, this is not possible. Instead, you must toenail the studs in place. To do so, drive nails at a 45-degree angle about 1 inch above the joint. When the nail is about ¼ inch into the wood, increase the angle to 60 or 70 degrees, and finish driving the nail. To keep studs from shifting when toenailing, use a temporary spacer block.

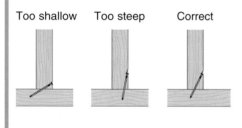

Too shallow   Too steep   Correct

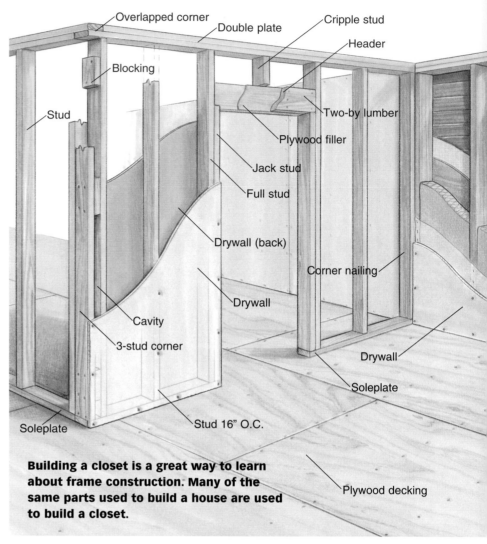

Building a closet is a great way to learn about frame construction. Many of the same parts used to build a house are used to build a closet.

Framing Basics

Find an area in a room where you don't need the floor space and where enclosing it would not impede traffic. If you can build the closet in a corner, you'll only need to build two walls. The closet's interior should be at least 24 inches deep and, for a bedroom closet, 48 inches wide.

Begin construction by marking the closet outline on the floor. Then nail down a 2x4 soleplate. Next, transfer the closet outline to the ceiling using a level or plumb line. The plumb line, a weighted string, allows you to find the precise location of the closet corner at the ceiling. Align the point of the plumb bob with the soleplate corner, and mark the corresponding spot on the ceiling. Then proceed to mark

for the top plate and attach using nails. Mark the top and bottom plate for the door. It should be the door width (from outside jamb edge to outside jamb edge) plus 1 inch.

Nail outside studs to existing walls. Then set inside studs 16 inches on center, and toenail them to the top plate and soleplate on all four sides. On each side of the door opening, nail a full stud and a jack stud. Place a header, constructed of two pieces of 2x6 lumber with ½-inch plywood filler between them, atop the jack studs. The jack stud height should be the height of the prehung door (to the top of the head jamb) plus ½ inch. Cut away the soleplate inside the doorway, and proceed to drywalling.

How To: Frame a Closet

1 Snap chalk lines for the locations of the top and bottom plates. Attach using nails.

2 Install end studs that abut existing walls. Attach closet studs to wall studs.

3 Mark every 16 in. from the first stud on the top and bottom plates. Strike lines at each mark.

4 Draw an X to the side of the line where the stud will go to avoid confusion later.

5 Toenail the studs into the plates. (See the "Smart Tip" on the opposite page.)

6 Preassemble a 3-stud corner; position it plumb; and nail it between the top and bottom plates.

7 Nail jack studs on each side of the closet doorway to carry the header.

8 Remove the section of soleplate in the doorway so you can run finished flooring into the closet space.

9 Install drywall inside and out; finish and sand the joints; prime; and paint.

For small drywall jobs, such as a closet, use a cordless drill (below). For larger jobs, a drywall screwdriver is faster and easier. Stir drywall compound thoroughly (bottom) before using.

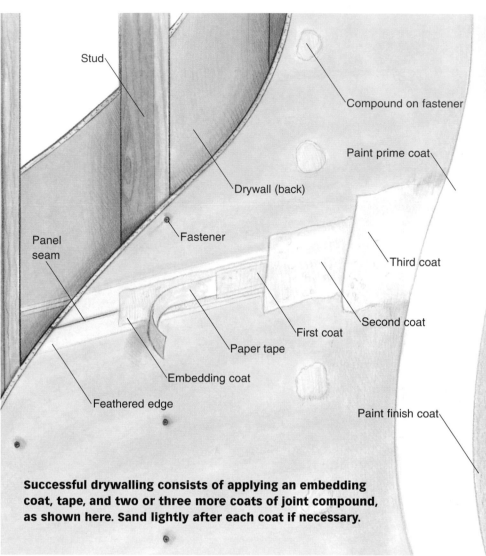

Stud

Compound on fastener

Paint prime coat

Drywall (back)

Fastener

Panel seam

Third coat

Second coat

First coat

Paper tape

Embedding coat

Feathered edge

Paint finish coat

Successful drywalling consists of applying an embedding coat, tape, and two or three more coats of joint compound, as shown here. Sand lightly after each coat if necessary.

Drywall Basics

Gypsum drywall may be used to cover the closet walls, inside and out. It's a good practice to sketch out a plan on paper to determine how to arrange the drywall panels and to estimate how much drywall you will need. It's not fun getting rid of extra drywall if you buy too much. Try to incorporate as many full sheets, horizontally positioned, in your plan as possible.

The preferred fasteners for drywalling today are drywall screws. Spacing requirements on walls are every 16 inches instead of the standard 8 inches for nails. Drywall screws are stronger than nails, less damaging to panels, and quicker to install. Fewer fasteners also speeds finishing.

Sanding between coats is only necessary if you've left ridges or raised spots while applying compound. Skilled drywall tapers can get by with little or no sanding.

How To: Finish Drywall Seams

1 Use a 4-in. taping knife to cover the heads of fasteners with dry-wall compound.

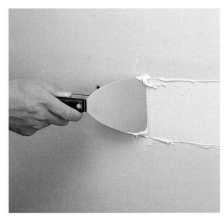

2 Use the same knife to spread a base coat on joints. This creates a bed for the paper joint tape.

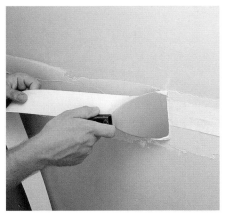

3 Guide the paper joint tape into the compound with one hand while smoothing with the knife.

4 Smooth with a 6-in. knife, using firm pressure, but don't squeeze the compound out from under the tape.

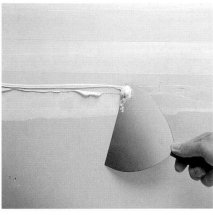

5 When the tape is smooth, run the knife along both sides of the joint to remove excess compound.

6 Sand dried compound over the fasteners using 120-grit sandpaper wrapped around a wood block.

7 When joints are dry, use a 10-in. knife to apply the first coat of compound; allow to dry; and sand.

8 Apply a second, wider coat, and sand. Apply a third coat if necessary to feather compound to drywall.

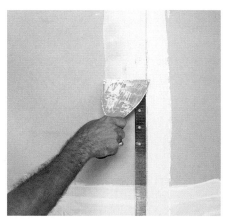

9 Use a metal corner guard on the corners. The bead will guide the knife when you apply compound.

Space Saver

Pocket doors save valuable space by sliding on a track directly into a cavity in the wall (the space normally filled with studs). They eliminate the need to swing a door through a room or hallway. They also save wall space. When you open a conventional door, it covers the wall and prohibits you from putting a chair or chest there. Install pocket doors according to the manufacturer's directions, and remember: the frame must be plumb for the door to slide smoothly on its track.

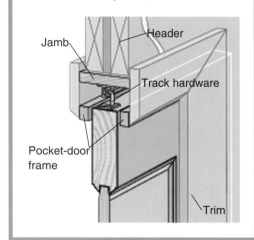

The key to successfully hanging a door is to make the side jambs plumb and the head jamb level.

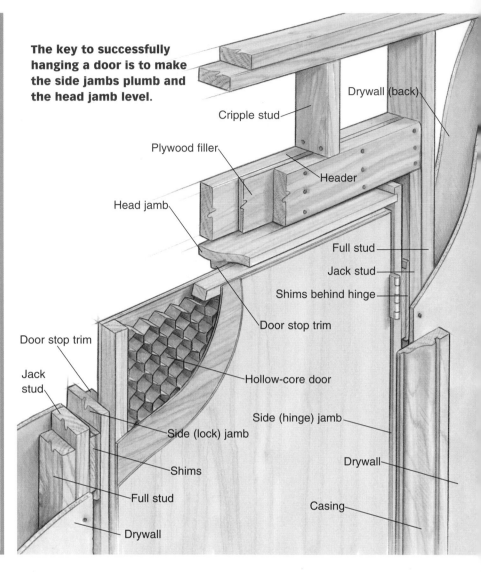

Hinged Door Basics

When adding a door to a closet, select a prehung unit. It will eliminate the need to fit the door to the opening, cut hinge and lockset mortises, and fit the stops.

Begin your installation. Remove the door from the frame by knocking out the hinge pins. Stand the frame (jambs) in the opening, and check that the head jamb is level. If one side is higher than the other, block up the low side jamb until it is correct, and note the thickness of the blocking required. Mark the bottom of the longer jamb (the one on the high side) this amount, and saw it off.

Place the frame in the opening again to make sure the head jamb is now level. Next, check whether or not the jack stud on the hinge side of the door is plumb. If it is, use 8d or 10d finishing nails to attach the top of the hinge-side jamb to the jack stud. Then place the level on the edges of the jamb to make sure it is vertical in both directions (plumb).

Adjust the jambs. If necessary, adjust the hinge jamb using shims, as shown in the photos on the opposite page. Place shims at the top, middle, and bottom. Once plumb, nail the jamb to the jack stud. Drive nails in pairs, side by side, through the shims. Next, rehang the door and adjust the lock jamb's position to achieve a $\frac{1}{16}$-inch clearance between the door edge and the jamb. Use shims as necessary. Finally, nail off the lock jamb.

How To: Install a Prehung Door

1 Check the opening for level and plumb. Tighten gaps between studs and drywall with screws.

2 Check that the jambs are square. If not, loosen the diagonal brace, adjust, and renail.

3 Tip the door unit into place so that the braces bear against the wall. Insert shims to hold the door in place.

4 After leveling and nailing the head jamb in place, tack nail the hinge jamb in place. Check for plumb.

5 Insert shims in pairs every 16 in. until plumb. Tap opposing shims to make fine adjustments.

6 Nail off the hinge jamb with finishing nails. Then plumb the opposite jamb using the same method.

7 When plumb, nail off the lock-side jamb. Score shims with a utility knife, and snap off excess.

8 Check the door for proper orientation. When satisfied, fasten mitered casing trim to the jambs.

9 Install a lockset in the predrilled hole, following the manufacturer's directions.

Options: "Found" Spaces for Closets

Valuable storage space may be untapped only because it's not where you expect it to be. Take a good look around, however, and you'll see that it *is* possible to find more storage space, even in smaller homes or apartments. Look up. The open space above kitchen cabinets—ideal for large bowls, pitchers, baskets, and serving trays—often goes unused. Look down. Toe kicks at the bottom of a base cabinet give you additional storage space for table linens, baking sheets, and other items. If you need every inch of storage space you can get, you may want to consider some unusual spots.

2 This luggage closet made use of underutilized attic space. When using "found" space in attics, don't forget to insulate the new closet walls and ceiling.

1 The sliver of space at the entry to this walk-in closet is just big enough for a cubby module. It abuts a built-in dresser and is a great place to store lotions, soaps, and colognes.

3 A narrow pullout organizer—this one is less than 3 in. wide—allows you to store items that are ill suited for shelves, such as keys, on hooks and pegs. Install at the end of a cabinet run.

How To: Create a Closet in Inches of Space

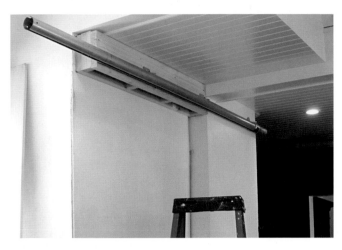

This slender pantry found a home in a space that measures only 6 in. deep. The header (above), was constructed of 2x8s and fastened to the wall studs with lag screws. Wall-mounted door hardware was used to hang the sliding door, which in a former life was an old stall gate from a horse barn.

Finding "Leftover" Space for Closets

In the typical home, there are unused spaces that can be used for closets. A good eye and a ruler may be all you need to discover hidden cavities behind walls, especially beside plumbing chases, flues, and fireplaces—as well as in adjacent rooms, such as attics and garages. You may also find usable space beneath (and above) stairs, and beside cabinets. Do not use spaces outside the insulation envelope of the house. Attic eaves, for example, may be off-limits because the knee walls are insulated and the space behind them is needed for ventilation.

Leftover space beneath stairs is typically the easiest to reclaim for storage.

Resource Guide

This list of manufacturers and associations is meant to be a general guide to additional industry and product-related sources. It is not intended as a listing of products and manufacturers represented by the photographs in this book.

Albed

Delmonte s.r.l.
Via San Martino 8
20054 Nova Milanese (MI) Italy
Phone: +39 0362 367112
www.albed.it/en/home.htm
An Italian company that designs and produces aluminum and glass walk-in closets. It also designs doors, bookcases, tables, and other accessories.

Association of Closet and Storage Professionals (ACSP)

214 N. Hale St.
Wheaton, IL 60187
Phone: 630-510-4590
www.closets.org
A national organization whose members provide professional help when installing a closet or storage solution. Its Web site includes images, tips on planning a closet and selecting a professional, and information to help you find a pro in your area.

California Closets

610A DuBois St.
San Rafael, CA 94901
Phone: 415-256-8500
www.californiaclosets.com
A company that designs and installs custom walk-in closets, reach-in closets, and freestanding wardrobes. Its storage accessories include baskets, tie racks, valet rods, and drawer dividers.

ClosetMaid

650 SW 27th Ave.
Ocala, FL 34474
Phone: 352-622-3907
www.closetmaid.com
A company that manufactures storage and organization products, including pullout shelves, storage towers, shoe cubbies, and cabinet organizers.

The Container Store

500 Freeport Pkwy., Ste. 100
Coppell, TX 75019
Phone: 888-266-8246
www.containerstore.com
Retail stores, located nationwide, that offer a wide range of space-saving products, including hanging sweater bags, adjustable garment racks, and hangers. The Web site offers tips for turning a closet into an office and planning a closet makeover.

Eco-Nize Closets

7500 Clifton Rd.
Clifton, VA 20124
Phone: 888-326-6493
www.eco-nize.com
A company that designs, builds, and installs customized eco-friendly closet systems, garage systems, pantries, and more for people in the mid-Atlantic region. It also offers a selection of organization accessories.

Eva-Dry

12157 W. Linebaugh Ave., Unit 152
Tampa, FL 33626
Phone: 877-382-3790
www.eva-dry.com
A company that manufactures renewable dehumidifiers that remove moisture from closets and cabinets. The dehumidifiers, which operate without electricity or batteries, eliminate mold, mildew, and moisture damage.

Flexco

1401 E. 6th St.
Tuscumbia, AL 35674
Phone: 800-633-3151
www.flexcofloors.com
A company that develops resilient, low-maintenance flooring, including rubber tile and solid vinyl tile. Its FlexTuft line is made from recycled tires and withstands high traffic and exposure to the elements.

Get Organized, Inc.

4380 36th St.

Orlando, FL 32811

Phone: 800-881-1553

www.getorganizedinc.com

A company that manufactures, sells, and installs customized cabinetry and shelving for closets (melamine and wood), pantries, garages, and more.

IKEA

Phone: 877-345-4532

www.ikea.com

An in-store and mail-order retailer of a wide range of cabinetry, appliances, and home furnishings at affordable prices. Offers an array of storage solutions, including customizable wardrobes, clothes racks, shelves, and hangers.

John Sterling Corp.

11600 Sterling Pkwy.

Richmond, IL 60071

Phone: 800-367-5726

www.johnsterling.com

A company that manufactures closet hardware products, including adjustable closet rods, closet pole sockets, shelf and rod brackets, and over-the-door garment rails.

Johnson Hardware

2100 Sterling Ave.

Elkhart, IN 46516

Phone: 800-837-5664

www.johnsonhardware.com

A company that manufactures door hardware for pocket doors, wall-mounted sliding doors, and bifold doors, among others.

Jokari Incorporated

1220 Champion Cr., No. 100

Carrollton, TX 75006

Phone: 214-237-0625

www.jokari.com

A company that produces storage and organization items, including bamboo over-the-door racks that hold sandals, caps, purses, backpacks, and other items.

Lema USA

Architects and Designers Building

150 E. 58th St., Floor 3

New York, NY 10155

Phone: 888-536-2872

www.lemausa.com

An Italian furniture company that manufactures wardrobes (freestanding or wall-mounted), closet systems, and wall units. All items are made in Italy to custom specifications.

Lutron

7200 Suter Rd.

Coopersburg, PA 18036

Phone: 888-588-7661

www.lutron.com

A company that offers thousands of lighting-control devices and wired and wireless systems, ranging from individual dimmers to total light-management systems that control an entire house.

MasterBrand Cabinets, Inc.

One MasterBrand Cabinets Dr.

P.O. Box 420

Jasper, IN 47547-0420

Phone: 812-482-2527

www.masterbrand.com

A company that manufactures all types of cabinetry under 13 different divisions, including Aristokraft, Decora, Diamond, Georgetown, Kemper, Kitchen Craft, Omega, and Somersby.

Maytag

240 Edwards St.

Cleveland, TN 37311

Phone: 800-688-9900

www.maytag.com

A company that manufactures a full line of kitchen and laundry appliances as well as heating and cooling systems for the home.

OnlineOrganizing.com

P.O. Box 655

Jackson, GA 30233

Phone: 877-251-8435

www.onlineorganizing.com

A Web-based company that offers a wide range of organizational and space-saving products (including a closet carousel), and provides free home and office organizing tips. You can sign up for free monthly newsletters on the Web site.

Playsam

P.O. Box 44
391 20 Kalmar, Sweden
Phone: +46 0480 411884
www.playsam.com
A Scandinavian design company whose Our Children's Gorilla brand makes the "apehanger" monkey clothes hanger, which is made of fiberboard with a nontoxic organic tint. The hangers come in red, black, brown, or yellow.

Poliform

Via Montesanto 28
22044 Inverigo (CO) Italy
Phone: +39 031 6951
www.poliform.it/index_en.html
An Italian furniture company that designs and produces high-end, contemporary wardrobes and walk-in closets.

The Pull-Out Shelf Company

POSCO Manufacturing, Inc.
3631 S. Broadmont Dr.
Tucson, AZ 85713
Phone: 520-299-2402
www.pulloutshelf.com
A company that custom builds and installs pullout shelf systems for pantries, broom closets, or storage closets. Slide-out units designed to fit around drains and pipes under the sink are also available.

Rev-A-Shelf

2409 Plantside Dr.
Jeffersontown, KY 40299
Phone: 800-626-1126
www.rev-a-shelf.com
A company that manufactures custom storage kits and organizing products for the home, including hard-to-find

items such as fold-out ironing boards, jewelry drawers, pullout closet mirrors, pull-down closet rods, valet rods, pivoting armoires, and a spiral clothes rack.

Rubbermaid

3320 W. Market St.
Fairlawn, OH 44333
Phone: 888-895-2110
www.rubbermaid.com
A company that manufactures household storage and organization products, including customizable closet kits, wire shelving, nestable bins, hanging shelf units, and over-the-door shoe organizers.

Schulte Corp.

3100 E. Kemper Rd.
Cincinnati, OH 45241
Phone: 513-277-3700
www.schultestorage.com

A company that produces specialty storage systems, including epoxy-coated wire shelving and the freedomRail line of adjustable storage for the home or garage. The freedomRail line is made with melamine and is offered in seven colors and finishes.

Solid Wood Closets, Inc.

815 Milford St.
Glendale, CA 91203
Phone: 800-351-9144
www.solidwoodclosets.com
A company that offers modular closet organizer systems made from eco-friendly hardwood, along with an assortment of closet accessories, including valet rods, jewelry drawers, and a scarf rack.

Stacks and Stacks

1045 Hensley St.
Richmond, CA 94801
Phone: 800-761-5222
www.stacksandstacks.com
An Internet company that offers more than 25,000 products for the home, office, garden, and automobile, including tie racks, shoe racks, over-the-door organizers, drawer dividers, garment racks, hangers, double-hang closet rods, shelf dividers, and complete closet organizer systems.

ViaBoxes.com

27600 S.E. Hwy. 212
Boring, OR 97009
Phone: 503-330-3033
www.viaboxes.com
A company that creates fun, functional furniture and storage for children. ViaBoxes are plywood storage cubes that stack or connect side by side to create different storage configurations. The cubes can be customized with doors, shelves, racks, drawers, and more.

Wood-Mode

One Second St.
Kreamer, PA 17833
Phone: 877-635-7500
www.wood-mode.com
A company that produces custom, semicustom, and standard cabinetry. It offers tilt-out bins, pullouts, recycling centers, and other specialized storage solutions.

Glossary

Anchor   A device, usually made of metal or plastic, inserted into walls and ceilings to provide support for fasteners of wall-mounted shelves and other storage units.

Bifold door   A hinged door, often used for closets, that folds into itself and slides on a head track to the side when opened.

Blocking   The installation of short pieces of lumber between joists or studs for supporting heavy objects.

Bottom plate   The horizontal framing member at the base of a wall.

Brad   A thin nail with a small, barrel-shaped head.

Bypass door   A unit of doors that slide past each other along tracks. These doors are commonly used in closets, although they allow access to only one side of the closet at a time.

Chifforobe   A tall, closet-like piece of furniture that typically has drawers on one side and space for hanging clothes on the other.

Cleat   A piece of wood or metal that is fastened to a structural member to support or provide a point of attachment for another member or fixture.

Closet carousel   A motorized organizer for walk-in closets. Clothes hang along the length of a conveyor, and with the push of a button, the carousel rotates along a track, allowing easy access to an entire wardrobe.

Contemporary   Any current design. The term is sometimes—and not always accurately—used to reference modern design.

Countersink   A bit or drill for making a funnel-shaped enlargement at the outer end of a drilled hole. Also, to make a countersink on (a hole), or to set the head of a screw at or below the fastened item's surface.

Cubic foot   A unit for measuring volume. One cubic foot, which is a cube with sides of 1 foot, equals 1,728 cubic inches.

Dado   A rectangular channel cut across the grain to make a joint in wood. Also, to provide with a dado.

Desiccant   A drying agent used to absorb moisture from the air.

Divider   A partition between separate spaces or areas. Dividers in drawers or drawer inserts help separate items.

Double hang   A space-maximizing setup in a closet in which two rods hang in a row vertically. One rod is typically 80–85 inches from the floor, and the other is 40–42 inches. This setup, which is also referred to as a "short hang," is ideal for shirts, suits, and folded pants.

Drawer insert   A device placed in a drawer that helps establish a spot for knives, spice containers, and other items. Also called a "drawer organizer."

Drywall   A paper-covered sandwich of gypsum used as a covering material for interior walls and ceilings. Also known as "wallboard" or "gypsum board."

Eave   The lower edge of a roof that overhangs a wall.

Epoxy coating   A durable baked-on finish used on wire shelves and related components.

Feathering   A technique for creating a smooth transition between joint compound and the drywall panel.

Finishing nail   A nail with a tiny round head, normally set below the surface of finished wood with a nail set.

Fluorescent   A type of light containing a phosphor that attracts ultraviolet light and converts it into visible light.

Footprint   The area on a surface covered by something.

Freestanding closet   A closet that is not attached to or supported by anything. Freestanding closets are less expensive and less permanent than framing a new closet from scratch. Also known as a "freestanding wardrobe."

Header   The thick horizontal structural member that runs above rough openings, such as doors and windows, in a building frame.

Helper shelf   A space-saving device that provides a second shelf above an existing one and prevents overstacking. Also known as a "half shelf."

Incandescent   A type of lamp that heats a tungsten filament to incandescence in order to give off light.

Jamb   A board that fits into door and window openings, covering the rough framing.

Jig   A device used to maintain the correct positional relationship between a piece of work and the tool.

Joist   A horizontal member in house framing that supports a floor or ceiling.

Laminate   A hard-surface, thin material made from melamine under high pressure and used for the finished surfaces of cabinets.

Lazy Susan   An axis-mounted shelf, usually installed in a corner cabinet, that rotates 360 degrees, thereby bringing many stored items within easy reach.

LED lighting Long-lasting lighting that conserves electricity. LED stands for "light-emitting diode."

Linear feet Length, in feet, along a straight line.

Linen Cloth made of flax and noted for its strength. Also, bed sheets, tablecloths, napkins, and other household articles made of linen cloth or a similar fabric.

Medium-density fiberboard (MDF) An engineered product made from compressed wood fibers and used in the construction of cabinets and shelves.

Melamine A durable plastic often used to produce laminate surfaces for composite materials.

Miter box An open-top square box with precut cut lines to guide angled or square saw cuts.

Modular Units of a standard size, such as pieces of a closet organizing system, that can be fitted together.

Mortise A hole cut into a piece of wood to receive another piece, such as a tenon, hinge, or lock set.

Mudroom A room, often located near the kitchen, for the shedding of dirty or wet footwear and clothing.

Murphy bed A bed that can be folded into a closet.

National Electrical Code (NEC) Body of regulations spelling out safe, functional electrical procedures. Local codes can add to but not delete from NEC regulations.

On center The distance between the centers of regularly spaced structural members, such as wall studs.

Over-the-door organizer A storage device that attaches to the back of a door with hardware or just hangs over the door. Great for shoes, hats, purses, and so forth.

Pantry A storage room or large cabinet for packaged goods.

Particleboard A material composed of wood chips and coarse fibers bonded with adhesive into large sheets from ½ to 1⅛ inches thick.

Pilot hole A hole drilled into a surface before a screw is inserted to prevent splitting.

Plumb Exactly vertical (in two planes).

Plumb bob A pointed metal weight with a string used to determine vertical alignment.

Plywood A structural material consisting of sheets of wood glued together, usually with the grains of adjacent layers arranged at right angles to provide strength.

Pneumatic nailer A tool that uses pressurized air to shoot nails into different surfaces.

Pocket door A door that slides into the wall. Pocket doors are a great option when there is no room for the swing of a hinged door.

Pullout A full-extension closet or cabinet component, such as a shelf, tray, bin, or rack, that is typically fitted with ball-bearing slides for ease of operation.

Reach-in closet A closet that is not large enough to enter.

Recessed light fixtures Light fixtures that are installed into ceilings, walls, or cabinets and are flush with the surrounding areas.

Setback The legally required distance of a structure or some other feature from the property line.

Shaker A type of plain-paneled cabinetry that has been inspired by the simple, utilitarian furniture made by the Shakers, an eighteenth-century religious sect.

Shim A narrow wedge of wood driven between two items to support, level, or adjust one of the items.

Soleplate The horizontal two-by lumber that forms the base of a framed wall. Also called "bottom plate."

Standard A vertical support structure that typically hangs from a hanger rail and is screwed onto a door or closet wall. It can hold shelves, racks, baskets, and other closet organization elements.

Stud A vertical member in a frame wall.

Substrate Any material that supports another material that is bonded over it.

Tack nail To nail one structural member to another temporarily with a minimal amount of nails.

Telescoping The movement of one part sliding out from another, lengthening an object. Telescoping closet rods allow for expansion or contraction as needed.

Tiered shelf A space-saving device that stores items on several levels or "steps."

Toe kick The narrow space below a base cabinet.

Toenail To drive a nail at an angle into the face of a board so it penetrates another board above or below it.

Top plate The framing member(s) on top of a stud wall, upon which joists rest.

Universal design Products and designs that are easy to use by people of all ages, heights, and physical abilities.

Valet rod An extendable rod that mounts to the wall or closet system and provides a place to hang dry-cleaned clothes or tomorrow's outfit.

Veneer A thin piece or section of wood, typically a layer of plywood, used as a surface material.

Walk-in closet A closet that is deep enough to allow a person to enter it.

Index

A

Attic storage, 141, 148–149

B

Basement storage, 120–121
Bed and bath linens, 86–87
Bifold doors, 34, 73
Bins, 18, 72, 123–124
Broom closets, 118–119
Bulk supplies, 118
Bypass doors, 34

C

Cabinets, 32
Clearing clutter, 11–13, 64, 89
Closets
    accessibility, 75
    back door, 48–51
    broom, 118
    carousel, 82
    colors, 20
    conventionally framed, 139
    custom, 33
    doors, 34–35
    drywalling, 144–145
    fold-out, 16
    for coats, 44–47
    for older children, 61–63
    for teens, 64–65
    for young children, 55–57
    framing, 142–143
    freestanding, 16, 76, 107–109, 137
    from a spare bedroom, 139
    front door, 46–47
    guest, 83
    hall, 85, 89
    in found spaces, 138
    island, 32, 67
    laundry, 131, 134–135
    linen, 85–91
    mirror, 15
    mudroom, 48–51
    office, 127, 133–135
    open, 17, 137–138, 140

    organizing systems, 36–43
    reach-in, 17, 72–74
    roll-out, 16
    rooms in, 134
    rotating, 16
    shelves, 23–24, 28, 41–42, 67, 86, 89, 104
    specialty, 127
    utility, 117
    walk-in, 16, 78–81
Clothes moth
    prevention, 71
Clothes rack, 113
Coat closets, 44–47
    building, 52–53
Coat rack, 112
Crafts, 128–130
Cubbies, 24, 50, 57, 70, 148
Curtained doors, 35, 73
Custom closets, 33

D

Dehumidifier, 21
Dimensions
    reach-ins, 73
Dividers, 19
Doors
    installing, 146–147
Double hang, 18, 24, 47, 69, 74, 81
Drawers, 32, 72, 118
    for pantries, 102–103
Drywalling, 144–145

F

Fiberboard system, 37–39
    installing, 39
Framing, 142–143
Freestanding wardrobes, 16, 76, 107–109, 137
French doors, 35

G

Garage storage, 120–122
Garments
    height allowances, hanging, 68
    stack heights, 69
    widths, 68, 75
Guest closets, 83

H

Hampers, 74
Hangers, 26–27
    for kids, 57
Hatboxes, 77
Hinged single doors, 34
Holiday items
    storage of, 97, 132
Hooks, 18, 29, 62

I

Ironing boards, 14

J

Jewelry
    storage for, 14, 32, 70
Junk drawer, 118

L

Laminate, 37–38
Laundry closets, 131, 134–135
Lighting, 20–21, 134
    clearances, 21
    safety, 20
    solar, 20
    switches, 21

M

Mirror
    for closets, 15
Moths, 71
Mudroom, 48–51
Murphy bed, 134–135

O

Office closets, 127, 133–135

Office supplies, 132

Off-season storage, 82

Organization theory, 14–15

Over-the-door organizers, 19, 47, 114–115

P

Pantries
in a cabinet, 94–95
in a found space, 149
reach-in, 94
storage strategies, 97–99
walk-in, 93–94

Pegs, 29, 62

Pocket doors, 35, 51, 73, 146

Pot rack, 112–113

Pull-down closet rods, 25, 58, 62

Pullouts
installing, 31
racks, 18, 68, 70, 74
trays and shelves, 30–31

R

Rail-and-standard system, 42–43

Reach-in closets, 17, 72–74

separate, 74
shared, 73–74

Rods, 24–25
load capacity, 25
recommended heights, 55, 69, 75

S

Scrapbook station, 129

Security closets, 132

Shed storage, 124–125

Shelves, 23–24, 28, 41–42, 67, 86, 89, 104
hardware, 28
helper, 98, 100–101
recommended widths, 69
revolving, 30
tiered, 98, 100–101

Shoes
maintenance of, 70
organizers, 59, 65, 70
racks for, 45, 59

Sliding doors, 34, 74, 83, 149

Solar closet lighting, 20

Specialty closets, 127

Steamer trunk wardrobe, 60

Storage
labeling, 53, 70, 72, 77, 89, 97, 132

Substrate, 37–38

T

Table linens, 85

Toys and games, 132

Track-and-hook system, 120–121, 124

U

Universal design, 75

Utility closets, 117

V

Vacuum, 118–119

Valet rod, 68

W

Walk-in closets, 16, 78–81
separate, 79
shared, 78

Wall-mount doors, 35, 149

Wall studs
locating, 28, 42

Wardrobe, 107–108
building components for, 110–111

Wheelchair access, 75

Wine cellar, 104–105

Wire systems, 40–43, 73

Credits

page 1: courtesy of California Closets **page 2:** courtesy of Rubbermaid **page 7:** courtesy of The Container Store **page 8:** courtesy of ClosetMaid **page 9:** top courtesy of Schulte; bottom courtesy of Rubbermaid **page 10:** courtesy of Poliform **page 11:** left courtesy of California Closets; right iStockphoto **page 12:** courtesy of The Container Store **page 13:** courtesy of Apple **page 14:** top courtesy of Lisa Adams/LA Closet Design; bottom left & bottom right courtesy of Rev-A-Shelf **page 15:** left & center courtesy of Rev-A-Shelf; right courtesy of MasterBrand **page 16:** left courtesy of IKEA; right courtesy of Rev-A-Shelf **page 17:** top left & right courtesy of Rubbermaid; bottom left courtesy of Johnson Hardware **page 18:** top left, top center, bottom left & bottom center courtesy of The Container Store; top right iStockphoto; bottom right courtesy of Rev-A-Shelf **page 19:** top left courtesy of Lema; top right courtesy of The Container Store; bottom courtesy of Jokari **page 20:** left courtesy of Poliform; right Shutterstock **page 21:** top left courtesy of Lutron; bottom left & bottom center courtesy of VELUX; bottom right courtesy of Eva-Dry **page 22:** courtesy of Lema **page 23:** left courtesy of Solid Wood Closets; right Mark Samu **page 24:** top left courtesy of Rev-A-Shelf; top center & bottom courtesy of Stacks and Stacks; top right courtesy of Eco-Nize Closets **page 25:** left courtesy of Eco-Nize Closets; right courtesy of Rev-A-Shelf **page 26:** top left & top right Shutterstock; bottom Home & Garden Editorial Services **page 27:** courtesy of IKEA **page 28:** left courtesy of Lema; top right courtesy of Rubbermaid; bottom right courtesy of John Sterling **page 29:** iStockphoto **page 30:** left courtesy of Rev-A-Shelf; top right & middle right courtesy of The Pull-Out Shelf Company; bottom right Carl Weese **page 31:** Carl Weese **page 32:** top left courtesy of Poliform; bottom left courtesy of Rev-A-Shelf; right courtesy of California Closets **page 33:** Richard Wolf **page 34:** courtesy of John-

son Hardware **pages 35–36:** courtesy of California Closets **page 37:** top courtesy of California Closets; middle courtesy of IKEA; bottom Home & Garden Editorial Services **page 38:** courtesy of Stacks and Stacks **page 39:** Mark Samu **page 40:** left Home & Garden Editorial Services; right courtesy of Schulte **page 41:** bottom right courtesy of Schulte; all others Home & Garden Editorial Services **page 42:** Home & Garden Editorial Services **page 43:** top courtesy of The Container Store; bottom courtesy of Schulte **page 44:** courtesy of ClosetMaid **page 45:** top courtesy of ClosetMaid; bottom Shutterstock **page 46:** courtesy of ClosetMaid **page 47:** courtesy of California Closets **page 48:** left courtesy of MasterBrand; top right iStockphoto; bottom right courtesy of California Closets **page 49:** courtesy of California Closets **page 50:** courtesy of Rubbermaid **page 51:** top courtesy of Rubbermaid; bottom courtesy of Johnson Hardware **page 52:** Lars Dalsgaard **page 53:** top left, top right & middle right Lars Dalsgaard; bottom right courtesy of Flexco **page 54:** courtesy of California Closets **page 55:** left Mark Samu; right iStockphoto **page 56:** top courtesy of Rubbermaid; bottom courtesy of The Container Store **page 57:** top courtesy of Playsam; bottom left & bottom right courtesy of ViaBoxes.com **page 58:** courtesy of Lisa Adams/ LA Closet Design **pages 59–60:** Lars Dalsgaard **page 61:** courtesy of Schulte **page 62:** courtesy of California Closets **page 63:** Mark Samu **page 64:** courtesy of California Closets **page 65:** top left & top right courtesy of IKEA; bottom left courtesy of California Closets **page 66:** courtesy of Lisa Adams/LA Closet Design **page 67:** top left courtesy of Schulte; bottom left & bottom right courtesy of California Closets **page 68:** courtesy of Rev-A-Shelf **page 70:** top left courtesy of Rubbermaid; top right courtesy of Lisa Adams/LA Closet Design; bottom left Shutterstock; bottom center courtesy of Rev-A-Shelf; bottom right courtesy of Lema **page 71:** Home & Garden Editorial Services **page 72:** left courtesy of The Container Store; top right courtesy of Schulte; middle right courtesy of Rubbermaid; bottom right courtesy of IKEA **page 73:** left courtesy of The Container Store; right Shutterstock **page 74:** top left courtesy of Rubbermaid; bottom left courtesy of Eco-Nize Closets; right courtesy of California Closets **page 75:** top left courtesy of Poliform; top right courtesy of IKEA; bottom right courtesy of Sears, Roebuck and Co. **page 76:** courtesy of IKEA **page 77** Shutterstock **page 78:** courtesy of California Closets **page 79:** top left & top right courtesy of California Closets; bottom right courtesy of Rubbermaid **page 80:** left courtesy of Poliform; right courtesy of Rubbermaid **page 82:** courtesy of OnlineOrganizing.com **page 83:** courtesy of Schulte; **page 84:** courtesy of ClosetMaid **page 85:** top left courtesy of Johnson Hardware; top right iStockphoto; bottom right courtesy of Schulte **page 86:** left courtesy of Schulte; right iStockphoto **page 87:** top courtesy of Jokari; bottom courtesy of Rev-A-Shelf **page 88:** courtesy of Lema **page 89:** left courtesy of Poliform; right iStockphoto **page 90:** courtesy of IKEA **page 91:** top iStockphoto; bottom Shutterstock **page 92:** courtesy of Schulte **page 93:** left Mark Samu; right courtesy of Schulte **page 94:** left courtesy of ClosetMaid; right courtesy of Wood-Mode **page 95:** top iStockphoto; bottom

Terra Ambridge **page 96:** left courtesy of Wood-Mode; top right courtesy of Merillat; bottom right courtesy of Kitchens by Deane **page 97:** courtesy of Rubbermaid **page 99:** courtesy of California Closets **pages 100–101:** Carl Weese **page 102:** top left courtesy of IKEA; bottom left courtesy of Wood-Mode; right Carl Weese **page 103:** Carl Weese **page 104:** top courtesy of Whirlpool; bottom courtesy of KitchenAid **page 105:** top left & top right courtesy of Maytag; bottom courtesy of California Closets **pages 106–107:** courtesy of IKEA **page 108:** top left Mark Samu; top right courtesy of IKEA; bottom right iStockphoto **pages 109–111:** Lars Dalsgaard **page 112:** top left iStockphoto; top right courtesy of Stacks and Stacks; bottom right courtesy of Rogar Intl. Corp. **page 113:** top left courtesy of Lisa Adams/LA Closet Design; top right courtesy of The Container Store; bottom left Home & Garden Editorial Services; bottom right courtesy of IKEA **page 114:** left & bottom right Home & Garden Editorial Services; top right courtesy of Rubbermaid **page 115:** top sequence courtesy of Jokari; bottom right Home & Garden Editorial Services **page 116:** courtesy of California Closets **page 117:** top left & right courtesy of Schulte; bottom left courtesy of California Closets **page 118:** left Carl Weese; top right & bottom right courtesy of Rubbermaid **page 119:** Mark Samu **pages 120–121:** courtesy of Rubbermaid **page 122:** courtesy of ClosetMaid **page 123:** top courtesy of Rubbermaid; bottom courtesy of Schulte **page 124:** left Robert Perron; right courtesy of Rubbermaid **page 125:** top Home & Garden Editorial Services; bottom left & bottom right courtesy of Rubbermaid **page 126:** courtesy of Johnson Hardware **page 127:** top courtesy of California Closets; bottom courtesy of Schulte **page 128:** courtesy of California Closets **page 129:** top left & top right courtesy of California Closets; bottom right courtesy of Schulte **page 130:** courtesy of Rubbermaid **page 131:** courtesy of The Container Store **page 132:** top courtesy of Rubbermaid; bottom courtesy of Schulte **page 133:** courtesy of California Closets **page 134:** courtesy of California Closets **page 135:** top left & bottom left Mark Lohman; middle left courtesy of California Closets; top right courtesy of The Container Store; bottom right courtesy of Lisa Adams/LA Closet Design **page 136:** Mark Samu **page 137:** left courtesy of IKEA; right Home & Garden Editorial Services **page 138:** top left, top right & bottom right courtesy of Poliform; bottom left courtesy of California Closets **page 139:** top courtesy of Poliform; bottom courtesy of Eco-Nize Closets **page 140:** top & middle courtesy of Albed; bottom courtesy of Poliform **page 141:** top courtesy of ClosetMaid; bottom courtesy of Poliform **page 143:** top right & middle left Brian C. Nieves; all others John Parsekian **page 144:** top courtesy of U.S. Gypsum; middle courtesy of Stanley Tools; bottom John Parsekian **page 145:** John Parsekian **page 147:** middle center & bottom left Neal Barrett; all others John Parsekian **page 148:** left Mark Lohman; top right Mark Samu; bottom right courtesy of Rev-A-Shelf **page 149:** top left, bottom left & top right Mark Samu; bottom right courtesy of California Closets **page 152:** courtesy of IKEA **page 157:** courtesy of Lema **page 158:** courtesy of California Closets

Have a home-improvement, decorating, or gardening project? Look for these and other fine **Creative Homeowner books** wherever books are sold.

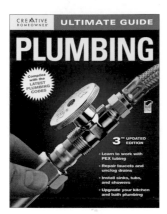

The complete manual for plumbing projects. Over 775 color photos and illustrations. 304 pp.; 8¹/₂" × 10⁷/₈"
BOOK #: CH278205

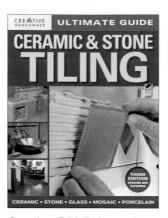

Complete DIY tile instruction. Over 550 color photos and illustrations. 240 pp.; 8¹/₂" × 10⁷/₈"
BOOK #: CH277525

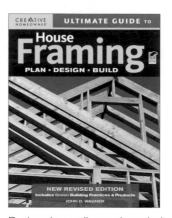

Designed to walk you through the framing basics. Over 750 photos and illos. 240 pp.; 8¹/₂" × 10⁷/₈"
BOOK #: CH277665

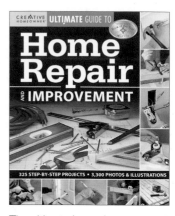

The ultimate home-improvement reference manual. Over 300 step-by-step projects. 608 pp.; 9" × 10⁷/₈"
BOOK #: CH267870

Complete source book for molding trim. 1,000+ color photos and illos. 256 pp.; 8¹/₂" × 10⁷/₈"
BOOK #: CH279402

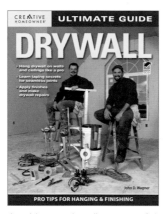

A guide covering all aspects of drywall. Over 450 color photos and illustrations. 176 pp.; 8¹/₂" × 10⁷/₈"
BOOK #: CH278330

Tips on gardening methods and selecting plants. Over 450 photos and illos. 256 pp.; 8¹/₂" × 10⁷/₈"
BOOK #: CH274183

Tips on everything from carpentry to landscaping. Over 500 photos and illos. 160 pp.; 8¹/₂" × 10⁷/₈"
BOOK #: CH267900

Inspiration for creating an attractive, up-to-date kitchen. Over 500 color photos. 224 pp.; 8¹/₂" × 10⁷/₈"
BOOK #: CH279412

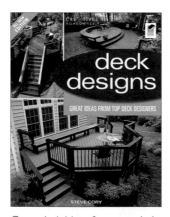

Great deck ideas from top designers. Over 450 color photos. 240 pp.; 8¹/₂" × 10⁷/₈"
BOOK #: CH277382

How to turn your yard into a small farm. Over 235 color photos and illos. 256 pp.; 8¹/₂" × 10⁷/₈"
BOOK #: CH274800

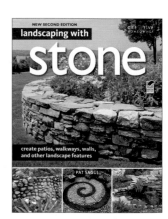

Ideas for incorporating stone into the landscape. Over 335 color photos. 224 pp.; 8¹/₂" × 10⁷/₈"
BOOK #: CH274179

For more information and to order direct, visit our Web site at **www.creativehomeowner.com**